The Power of Music

BY DON STADDON JR.

The Power of Music

Published by the Institute in Basic Life Principles
Box One
Oak Brook, IL 60522-3001
www.iblp.org

All Scripture verses are quoted from the
King James Version of the Bible.

Printed in the United States of America.

Layout and design by James Staddon
www.lenspiration.com

120203, 120204   1P   6/12

CONTENTS

DEDICATION

To Donna Staddon, my precious wife, who has earned a degree in music, has taught musical skills to all of our children, and has cheerfully and patiently helped me work out ways to explain technical musical concepts in layman's terms.

To Donald, Michael, Robert, Esther, James, Daniel, Jonathan, and David Staddon, our seven sons and one daughter who have sacrificially given hours of their time to review this book and offer countless improvements. James has also provided experienced leadership as a graphic designer in designing and publishing the book. It was worth writing this book just to have family time together and to gain their valuable perspectives.

To Dr. Bill Gothard, whose teaching in the *Basic Seminar* opened my eyes to the relevance of Scripture to every area of life, including the area of music. Subsequent teaching in the *Advanced Seminar* provided valuable additional insights for this book.

To Frank Garlock, whose video series *The Language of Music* reinforced my growing personal convictions on the morality of music.

To Loren Elms who provided a very useful list of references that proved so helpful in navigating the vast sea of information on the history of music.

To Francis Schaffer, whose book *Escape From Reason* helped me understand the serious effects that a false belief system can have on a culture.

To Donna Reese, our editor, who not only polished the language but also offered rich recommendations to help clarify some of the difficult ideas addressed in this book.

To Dennis Ondrovic and his publishing team for all their efforts to fit the proofing, printing, and binding processes into their busy schedule.

To the Holy Spirit, Who has gently reproved, corrected, and guided me through the Scriptures into a personal relationship with the Lord Jesus Christ. My desire is that this book will be a blessing to many for the glory of our musical Father which is in heaven.

Introduction

THE BIBLE IS THE FINAL AUTHORITY in all matters of life and practice. "If they speak not according to this word, it is because there is no light in them" (Isaiah 8:20). I have had the joy of learning with my family how life can be structured around every word that comes from the mouth of God. (See Matthew 4:4.) However, we have noticed—with distress—that there is a growing number of brothers and sisters in Christ who claim they are free to listen to any type of music. Based on this belief they state that believers should accept the way God speaks through different types of music.

Acceptance has an important and proper place in Christian charity, as the Apostle Paul said: "To the weak became I as weak, that I might gain the weak: I am made all things to all men, that I might by all means save some" (I Corinthians 9:22). However, in the same letter to the Corinthians, the Apostle Paul accurately discerned and condemned immoral actions: "For I verily, as absent in body, but present in spirit, have judged already, as though I were present, concerning him that hath so done this deed. In the name of our Lord Jesus Christ, when ye are gathered together, and my spirit, with the power of our Lord Jesus Christ, to deliver such a one unto Satan for the destruction of the flesh, that the spirit may be saved in the day of the Lord Jesus" (I Corinthians 5:3–5).

Paul objectively evaluated what was done in the church in light of divine revelation and made a righteous judgment. Because he accurately understood the behavior of this man at Corinth and evaluated that behavior in the light of God's divine nature, Paul drew the right conclusion. Paul's judgment was accurate and objective, not merely personal and subjective. In the same way, we may accurately understand the elements of music, evaluate them in the light of God's divine nature, and make an objective, righteous judgment.

> ... we can determine whether music is an amoral issue and consequently simply a matter of what we like or whether music is a moral issue and therefore a matter of what God is like.

If a child were about to eat even a small amount of candy-coated poison, would we not warn him of the danger rather than simply allow him to eat it ... just because he likes the flavor of the candy coating? Out of concern for others' well-being, we must sound the alarm when a moral issue is involved. Therefore, if we love God and desire His best in the matter of music, our first concern will be to answer this basic question: Is music moral (good or evil in God's sight) or amoral (morally neutral without consequences)?

This is where my study begins. By objectively opening our hearts to what God says in His Word, we can determine whether music is an amoral issue and consequently simply a matter of what we like or whether music is a moral issue and therefore a matter of what God is like.

If music is a moral issue, then it becomes our responsibility to discern on a case-by-case basis whether a piece of music is morally good or morally evil (immoral). Because there are hundreds of specific references to music in the Bible, as well as numerous general Biblical principles that relate to this subject, we can know what God says about music and discern whether or not different styles of music are consistent with His divine nature.

Because "the Spirit itself beareth witness with our spirit . . ." (Romans 8:16), moral truth about music is discerned primarily by one's spirit, not primarily by one's natural mind or emotions. (See also I Corinthians 2:14.) That is, one discerns in his spirit if a musical sound is acceptable unto the Lord by how close the characteristics of that music align with the characteristics of God's divine nature rather than by how close the characteristics of the music align with one's personal taste. The issue is not what we like—but what is God like.

Throughout this study, the term music refers primarily to musical sound rather than to words. The term lyrics is used when referring to words that may be sung with music.

The purpose of Section I of this book is to establish the principle that music is a moral issue. Section II will explore the characteristics of musical sound in the light of what Scripture reveals about God's divine nature so that we may readily identify music that is morally right or wrong. Section III will trace the Biblical origins of music and survey the history of Contemporary Christian Music (CCM) in the United States from a moral perspective. Finally, in Section IV we will conclude by observing how the power of music is influencing our culture for good or for evil.

SECTION I

The Morality of Music

SECTION I OF THIS BOOK presents the foundational principle of the morality of musical sound itself apart from the influence of lyrics. It is the musical nature of God that helps us objectively understand the moral nature of music. Therefore, Chapter 1 looks at the musical aspect of God's divine nature. Chapter 2 shows the power of musical sound to communicate a moral message. In this chapter we will see how the characteristics of the volume and order of music communicate a message that is either consistent or inconsistent with God's nature. We also will learn how the neutral (amoral) parts of music combine to form a moral message.

As the concept of the morality of music is presented to the mind, along with it may come some conviction to one's conscience. If this happens, the mind will tend to rush to the "rescue" of the conscience with rationalizations to justify one's personal preferences. Therefore, Chapter 3 concludes this section with answers to some of the common rationalizations given by those who reject the morality of music.

A Prayer for God's Perspective

"Teach me thy way, O Lord; I will walk in thy truth: unite my heart to fear thy name" (Psalm 86:11).

CHAPTER 1

God's Musical Nature

IN THIS CHAPTER WE WILL examine two aspects of God's divine nature: His strength and His song. Comparing these two attributes helps to establish a foundation for a proper evaluation of music. Remember, when a statement is verified two or three times in Scripture, a significant truth is established. (See Deuteronomy 19:15 and Matthew 18:16.)

This statement, "The LORD is my strength and song, and he is become my salvation," is repeated in three different major sections of the Old Testament. Exodus is in the section of the Law—Exodus 15:2, Psalms is in the section of Poetry—Psalm 118:14, and Isaiah is in the section of Prophecy—Isaiah 12:2. These passages establish the fact that the LORD's divine nature includes both strength and song! Note also that the passage in Exodus 15 documents the first song recorded in the Bible.

Strength is the first aspect of God's nature that is revealed in these three passages. He is omnipotent (all-powerful or all-strength). God is a Spirit. Therefore, to say that strength is an aspect of God's nature is to refer to a spiritual strength beyond any strength found in this physical world. To say "the LORD is my strength" means that the Lord is the One Who imparts His spiritual strength to me in the physical realm: His strength can become my strength.

Yet, God in His sovereignty allows strength and power to be exercised by men and evil spirits in the world in a way that resists His will and is contrary to His holy nature. Some examples are found in the following passages:

- "Ye . . . say, Have we not taken to us horns by our own strength?" (Amos 6:13).

- "Wherein in time past ye walked according to the course of this world, according to the prince of the power of the air, the spirit that now worketh in the children of disobedience" (Ephesians 2:2).

- "And in that same hour he cured many of their infirmities and plagues, and of evil spirits . . ." (Luke 7:21).

- "Who hath delivered us from the power of darkness, and hath translated us into the kingdom of his dear Son" (Colossians 1:13).

In history, Hitler and other dictators certainly used their God-given strength outside of God's ways. Clearly, there is a moral aspect to strength and power. Now consider what God thinks of the use of power that is contrary to His ways: "Thou shalt not suffer a witch to live" (Exodus 22:18); "Thou [God] lovest righteousness, and hatest wickedness . . ." (Psalm 45:7). Although God allows evil power, He hates the exercise of power that is outside of His ways and contrary to His holy nature.

For certain, He that is in us is greater than he that is in the world. (See I John 4:4.) But should we willingly associate with evil powers? God forbid. Rather, we are to abstain from all appearance of evil. (See I Thessalonians 5:22 and Romans 6:1–2.)

Song is the second aspect of God's nature that is revealed in these three passages. Here, the Hebrew word for *song* is *zimrath* (Strong's Concordance #2176), which means "instrumental music" and refers to musical sound. The only times this word occurs in the entire Bible are in these three passages. *Zimrath* describes song as an attribute of God's nature, just as strength is an attribute of His nature. God is musical! There is a musical aspect to His divine nature. As with the other attributes of God, to say that song is an aspect of God's nature is to refer to a spiritual song beyond any song found in this physical world.

> . . . to say that song is an aspect of God's nature is to refer to a spiritual song beyond any song found in this physical world.

God sings. Zephaniah says, "The Lord thy God in the midst of thee is mighty; he will save, he will rejoice over thee with joy; he will rest in his love, he will joy over thee with singing" (Zephaniah 3:17). Jesus also sang with His disciples. (See Matthew 26:30.)

Other passages that confirm the musical nature of God include these:

- "And the Lord shall be seen over them, and his arrow shall go forth as the lightning: and the Lord God shall blow the trumpet, and shall go with whirlwinds of the south" (Zechariah 9:14).

- "For the Lord himself shall descend from heaven with a shout, with the voice of the archangel, and with the trump of God: and the dead in Christ shall rise first" (I Thessalonians 4:16). Note that this is not the trumpet of angels but of God Himself.

- Psalms 113–118, 136 are called the "hallel songs." Note that Psalm 118 is one of the three passages listed at the beginning of this chapter. Historically, the *hallel* songs were part of the Jewish Passover. It is therefore quite possible that Jesus may have sung Psalm 118 at the Last Supper with His disciples, thus expressing in song that His Heavenly Father was His song. Furthermore, Christ would have been the most perfect expression of that song.

- "And I saw as it were a sea of glass mingled with fire: and them that had gotten the victory over the beast, and over his image, and over his mark, and over the number of his name, stand on the sea of glass, having the harps of God. And they sing the song of Moses the servant of God, and the song of the Lamb, saying, Great and marvelous are thy works, Lord God Almighty; just and true are thy ways, thou King of saints" (Revelation 15:2–3).

The fact that there is a musical aspect to God's nature establishes the moral aspect of music. "The LORD is my song" means that He imparts His spiritual song to me in the physical realm. His song can take on a physical dimension and become my song. God can express His song through me.

Just as God allows evil power, so in His sovereignty He allows evil music. He allows the world to sing its own song, a song that resists His will and is contrary to His holy nature. The following verses mention the songs of fools and of harlots:

"It is better to hear the rebuke of the wise, than for a man to hear the song of fools" (Ecclesiastes 7:5); ". . . After the end of seventy years shall Tyre sing as an harlot" (Isaiah 23:15). Additional Scripture showing that there is musical sound itself that is contrary to God's nature will be discussed in Chapter 5.

Just as God does not desire strength to be used in an unrighteous way, neither does He desire music to be sung or played in an unrighteous, worldly way. In Chapter 10 we will see how evil music is closely associated with evil power.

> The fact that there is a musical aspect to God's nature establishes the moral aspect of music.

Just as strength that is exercised contrary to God's nature becomes an evil power, so music that is arranged in an unrighteous way becomes unclean and is morally wrong. Just as we should not invite evil powers into our lives, so we should not invite evil music into our lives. It is true that we can block out evil music in our minds (e.g., while shopping in a store), but it is also true that we should not willingly invite evil music into our lives, our homes, or our churches.

Now consider a third aspect of God's nature that is revealed in these three passages. The Lord imparts His strength and His song to us in the same way that He imparts His salvation to us. We do not do good works and offer them up to God as a basis for salvation. Salvation originates within the heart of God and is offered to us as a gift. The same is true of His strength and His song. Strength and music flow from God's divine presence into our lives. The fact that music originates within the heart of God means that music is one of His divine characteristics. And because God is holy, the music that exists in His presence is holy and morally pure. Music is not amoral. Music is morally good or evil according to its agreement with or conflict with God's divine nature.

Based on the fact that God's nature is musical, do you want to listen to music that is in conflict with His nature? Most believers make a conscious effort to determine if the sermons they hear or the books they read are consistent with the nature of God and His truth as revealed in Scripture. Do you make the same conscious effort to determine if the musical sound itself is consistent with God's nature?

> Knowing what makes a musical style morally good or evil should be based objectively on its harmony with God's nature and design, not subjectively on personal preferences alone.

Knowing what makes a musical style morally good or evil should be based objectively on its harmony with God's nature and design, not subjectively on personal preferences alone. Scripture commands us to change our inclinations: "Set your affections [personal likes and dislikes] on things above, not on things on the earth. For ye are dead, and your life is hid with Christ in God" (Colossians 3:2–3).

Within the wide range of music that is morally acceptable unto the Lord, there is ample room for various styles of music and personal preferences. However, one of the purposes of this book is to draw attention to the need to first establish those moral bounds before deciding on personal preferences.

Do you want the music on which you set your affections to represent the evil lifestyle of the world or the divine pattern of things above? This is an important question, because the answer will have a direct effect on the way Christ is presented to the world. It may be that you have never seriously considered this question before. If not, carefully reconsider God's musical nature and the associated concepts presented in the following two chapters.

CHAPTER 2

Music's Moral Messages

IN THIS CHAPTER WE WILL LEARN about the power of moral messages contained within musical sound. To do this, we will first show how sound itself has the power to influence us. Second, we will demonstrate how musical sounds contain messages of their own, apart from lyrics. Third, we will see how the messages communicated by musical sound are morally good or evil. These messages are so powerful that they can overpower and even change the messages in the lyrics.

1. SOUND HAS POWER

Sound has the power to influence us physically. Police have actually used low-frequency sound cannons as weapons to injure or incapacitate subjects by using a focused beam of sound or ultrasound.[1]

Leonard Bernstein, an American composer and conductor, said: "Music doesn't have to pass through the censor of the brain before it can reach the heart . . . . An F-sharp doesn't have to be considered in the mind; it is a direct hit, and therefore, all the more powerful."[2] All of us have experienced the influence of musical sound. It inspires patriotism. It evokes reverence. It paralyzes with fear.

A Biblical demonstration of the power of sound occurred when God gave combat orders to Joshua: "And it shall come to pass, that when they make a long blast with the ram's horn, and when ye hear the sound of the trumpet, all the people shall shout with a great shout; and the wall of the city shall fall down flat, and the people shall ascend up every man straight before him" (Joshua 6:5). This is exactly what occurred later as recorded in Joshua 6:20. God worked through the power of sound to bring the walls tumbling down!

A Biblical example of how musical sound was used to accompany an evil purpose is given in the book of Daniel. Notice in this second Biblical example that the mention of music is a detail of high enough importance to God that He included it repeatedly in the inspired account. While this passage does not specifically address the morality of the music itself, it is certainly a warning about how music can be associated with and supportive of false worship: "Then an herald cried aloud, To you it is commanded, O people, nations, and languages, That at what time ye hear the sound of the cornet, flute, harp, sackbut, psaltery, dulcimer, and all kinds of musick, ye fall down and worship the golden image that Nebuchadnezzar the king hath set up: And whoso falleth not down and worshippeth shall the same hour be cast into the midst of a burning fiery furnace. Therefore at that time, when

> Music doesn't have to pass through the censor of the brain before it can reach the heart.

all the people heard the sound of the cornet, flute, harp, sackbut, psaltery, and all kinds of musick, all the people, the nations, and the languages, fell down and worshipped the golden image that Nebuchadnezzar the king had set up" (Daniel 3:4–7).

Another example of the powerful influence of sound was shown by a Suffolk, Virginia, high school student named David Merrill, who won top honors in regional and state science fairs by demonstrating the effects of music on lab mice. After the mice ran through a maze in about 10 minutes, Merrill played classical music to one group and heavy metal to another for 10 hours a day.

After three weeks, the mice exposed to classical music made it through the maze in 1½ minutes. The control group of mice to which no music was played made it through the maze in 5 minutes. The mice exposed to rock music took 30 minutes.

Said Merrill: "I had to cut my project short because all the hard-rock mice killed each other. None of the classical mice did that."[3]

2. MUSICAL SOUND COMMUNICATES MESSAGES

Musical sound has the power to influence our view of life and how we conduct ourselves. Because music bypasses the brain and directly influences the heart, some have called music the "language of emotion." For example, a lady walks up to a door, puts her key in the lock, opens the door, and walks in. There is nothing unusual about that scene—it happens thousands of times every day—unless you add the language of emotion.

Now, imagine that same scene in a movie . . . with suspenseful music playing in the background. We all have heard that type of sound, and without any words being spoken, we know someone or some thing is waiting behind that door.

Independent of whether that particular sound may or may not have been learned previously, it communicated an unspoken message that changed the whole meaning of the scene. When I hear an eerie sound, do I first think, "Now, that's an eerie sound; therefore I am going to make a decision to feel afraid"? No, the message is conveyed by the musical sound itself and is communicated directly to my emotions, apart from any words or conscious thought.

> . . . some have called music the "language of emotion."

Musical sound carries a message, and that message can have a powerful influence on us. Consider how some commercial jingles are remembered for years without the slightest mental effort and even the least desire to remember them.

Advertisers paid $100,000 per second for the 2011 Super Bowl commercials.[4] Would advertisers pay such prices for forms of media that were not effective in communicating their message?

A Biblical example of how sound communicated a message and altered behavior occurred when the Lord came down in the sight of all the people of Israel upon mount Sinai: "And it came to pass on the third day in the morning, that there were thunders and lightnings, and a thick cloud upon the mount, and the voice of the trumpet exceeding loud; so that all the people that was in the camp trembled" (Exodus 19:16). The verbal message from Moses was reinforced by the non-verbal messages of the thunder and the exceeding loud sound of the trumpet. The Israelites were influenced by the message in musical sound itself and trembled at the idea of approaching the boundary that God had set for them.

3. MUSICAL SOUND COMMUNICATES MORAL MESSAGES

Can musical sound communicate messages that are contrary to God's nature, outside of His design, and therefore against His will? A study of verbal languages indicates that the form in which ideas are expressed affects the meaning of those ideas. For example, if someone gives me a gift and I say "thanks" with a joyful smile, then I communicate acceptance and appreciation. If I say "thanks" with sarcasm (implying that I already have ten of those items), then I communicate indifference and rejection. The form (attitude) in which I express the word *thanks* can totally change the meaning communicated by that word.

The sociology of music is the study of music in relation to society. Kenneth A. Myers is a Christian author who has studied America's pop culture and documented his findings in *All God's Children and Blue Suede Shoes*. In his writings he demonstrates the significant influence that cultural forms can have on communication. Myers observes that the forms in which a culture expresses itself (e.g. art, music) can change and even cancel the content or meaning of the words that are

> . . . the form in which ideas are expressed affects the meaning of those ideas.

communicated. The form (attitudes, music) by which words are communicated can affect the meaning of what is communicated and change the meaning of the literal words that are used.

Experience tells us that musical sound itself communicates a message. To show how this message may be morally right or morally wrong, consider the form in which the words *Jesus Christ* may be spoken or sung. "Thou shalt not take the name of the LORD thy God in vain; for the LORD will not hold him guiltless that taketh his name in vain" (Exodus 20:7). There is nothing wrong with speaking God's name verbally or musically, but it would be morally wrong to speak it in vain.

The Hebrew word *vain* (#7723) means "false" (as in falsely representing God's nature) or "idolatrous" (as a false god). One way to misrepresent God's name would be to present it in an unholy "form." That form may be a personal attitude or a musical expression that is not consistent with God's holy nature. For example, the attitude in which Jesus Christ's name is spoken is a serious matter. It may communicate reverence, as Peter said: "In the name of Jesus Christ of Nazareth rise up and walk" (Acts 3:6), or it may communicate blasphemy in a curse. Paul gave a sharp warning to those who were carelessly allowing such blasphemy to occur in their worship services: "Wherefore I give you to understand, that no man speaking by the Spirit of God calleth Jesus accursed: and that no man can say that Jesus is the Lord, but by the Holy Ghost" (I Corinthians 12:3). Blasphemy occurs any time God's name is not reverenced the way it deserves to be reverenced.

Technically, the same words can be spoken, but the verbal message they carry may have entirely different meanings based on the attitude in which those words are spoken. The same is true of a musical form. In the song "O How I Love Jesus," the name of Jesus Christ is exalted. However, if a vocalist were to sing accurate words about the love of Jesus Christ but accompany those words with musical sounds characteristic of a sensual lover, then the musical message communicated by that song would be taking God's name in vain. Sensual musical forms change the meaning of the technically proper words (agape love), into a message that communicates something entirely "false" about Him (erotic love). Jesus is not an erotic god like the many "Playboy gods" of the Greeks and Romans. How false! How unthinkable! Such a message would be rejected as absolutely heretical if it appeared in print. However, such messages can and often do convey themselves with ease through the subtle untested language of music.

> ". . . if a vocalist were to sing accurate words about the love of Jesus Christ but accompany those words with musical sounds characteristic of a sensual lover, then the musical message communicated by that song would be taking God's name in vain."

In answer to the question posed at the beginning of this third point, it is clear that musical messages have the power to change the meaning of verbal messages. Although God in His sovereignty may allow unclean musical messages to corrupt clean verbal messages, He is not pleased. The LORD will not hold him guiltless that takes His name in vain.

Many are neither aware of nor willing to test the powerful emotional messages contained in musical sound, but choices have consequences. Based on the carnal messages in the musical sounds of much of American contemporary music, it is no wonder there is such breakdown in marriage, lack of self-control, and a general acceptance of immorality and perversion, both in society and in our churches. An unwillingness to evaluate the moral messages communicated in musical sounds reveals a deep-seated love for the world and its temporal pleasures.

In addition to the lyrics, are the moral messages in the music you listen to reflecting truths or lies about the nature of God? Will you purpose to listen only to musical styles that accurately reflect the true nature of God? He cares about the way you allow Him to sing through you.

Let's investigate two components of musical sound that can be manipulated in such a way as to make musical sound morally wrong.

The Moral Aspect of Volume

It is certainly exhilarating to sing aloud with our whole heart, and we should all sing heartily as to the Lord when we sing. Biblical examples of loud music include II Chronicles 30:21 (at a feast), Nehemiah 12:42 (at the dedication of a wall), and Psalm 150:5 (with loud cymbals).

Natural singing, even with full orchestral accompaniment at "full volume," is not damaging. However, when electronic amplifiers are used, that is not the case. There is an appropriate place for the use of electronic amplifiers. However, can the volume be increased so loud that it becomes wrong—morally wrong? The following Biblical principle applies to this question: "What? know ye not that your body [including your ears] is the temple of the Holy Ghost which is in you, which ye have of God, and ye are not your own?" (I Corinthians 6:19). "Know ye not that ye are the temple of God, and that the Spirit of God dwelleth in you? If any man defile [#5351: spoil, ruin, corrupt, destroy] the temple of God, him shall God destroy; for the temple of God is holy, which temple ye are" (I Corinthians 3:16–17).

God designed our bodies, and He created our ears to function properly within a limited range of volume. At what volume do the sound frequencies begin to damage the inner ear? The National Institute on Deafness and Other Communication Disorders states: "When we are exposed to harmful sounds that are too loud or that last a long time, sensitive structures in our inner ear can be damaged, causing noise-induced hearing loss (NIHL)."[5]

Sound is measured in units called decibels. The humming of a refrigerator is 45 decibels, normal conversation is approximately 60 decibels, and the noise from heavy city traffic can reach 85 decibels. "Long or repeated exposure to sounds at or above 85 decibels can cause hearing loss. The louder the sound, the shorter the time period before NIHL can occur. Sounds of less than 75 decibels, even after long exposure, are unlikely to cause hearing loss."[6]

In another study it was learned that sound broadcast at a level of 115 decibels for 15 minutes was damaging to the inner ear and that for every 5 decibels above that, the time of exposure required to cause damage was reduced by half (i.e., 120 db = 7½ min; 125 db = 3¾ min).[7]

At some point in a person's life, sound (musical sound) itself can become defiling (destructive, evil), and it becomes morally wrong to willfully listen to it at that volume. It is no longer a matter of what I may like; rather, it is a matter of what is appropriate for the temple of God and what pleases or displeases our loving Creator.

Can the effect of "loud" sounds in the damaging range be made morally acceptable by adding godly words to them? Obviously not; the sound itself is defiling and destructive apart from any words.

Would it be appropriate to use "loud," potentially damaging sounds (above the 75 decibel range) to identify with the lost in order to attract them to a religious meeting? No matter how sincere, the ends would not justify the means.

> Can the effect of "loud" sounds in the damaging range be made morally acceptable by adding godly words to them?

Hudson Taylor adopted cultural dress in order to identify with the Chinese, but he did not adopt immodest dress. We are commanded to attract people to Christ by light (that which is holy), not by darkness (that which is unholy). (See Matthew 5:16.)

Should we ever willingly and habitually expose ourselves to "loud," damaging music? Our Heavenly Father's answer is clear: "Abstain from all appearance of evil" (I Thessalonians 5:22).

"Thou shalt love the Lord thy God with all thine heart, and with all thy soul, and with all thy might. And these words, which I command thee this day, shall be in thine heart" (Deuteronomy 6:5–6). Let's not live on the edge of morality but rather move toward the center of God's love. Let's not look for a dangerous line but rather create a safe gap. As much as possible, move wholeheartedly toward God's best.

The Moral Aspect of Order

God is a God of order, and His order is seen throughout the created world, including the world of sound. As we resist God's order, the result is confusion, and God is not the author of confusion.

Let's observe the confusion that can result from disorder in sound itself, apart from words: "Now, brethren, if I come unto you speaking with tongues, what shall I profit you, except I shall speak to you either by revelation, or by knowledge, or by prophesying, or by doctrine? And even things without life giving sound, whether pipe or harp, except they give a distinction in the sounds, how shall it be known what is piped or harped? For if the trumpet give an uncertain sound, who shall prepare himself to the battle?" (I Corinthians 14:6–8).

In addressing an issue with "tongues" in verse six, Paul seeks to correct a communication problem. Paul states that the Corinthians would profit by his visit only if he communicated with them clearly through revelation, knowledge, prophesying, or doctrine.

What is significant in regard to music is the underlying principle about sound that Paul gives to support his point, in verse seven. The principle stated in verse seven is that "things without life giving sound" have the capacity to communicate messages that can be understood. Things without life include instruments such as the pipe and harp. Their sound has the power to communicate without lyrics. However, to avoid confusion there must be a distinction in the

> . . . confusion can result from disorder in sound itself, apart from words.

sounds. The Greek word *distinction* (#1293) means "variation" or "difference." In the context of this passage it means to be clearly this or clearly that; distinguishing one sound from another and eliminating confusion between the sounds.

Paul is basing his argument on a self-evident truth. Sound itself carries a message, and that message has consequences. It may result in order, or it may result in confusion.

In verse eight Paul illustrates the general principle with the specific example of the sound of a trumpet in battle. If the trumpet, which is now a third instrument separate from the pipe or harp, "give an uncertain sound," who shall prepare himself to the battle? The Greek word for *uncertain* (#82) means "indistinct" or "confusing." An indistinct sound (apart from any words) in battle will communicate an indistinct message to the soldiers, resulting in great confusion and possible loss of life. The sound itself communicates a message that is either clear or confusing.

Note how the serious consequences of an uncertain sound are independent of the sincerity of the one sounding the trumpet. Paul's point is that sound itself, apart from lyrics and motives, carries a message, and that message has the potential of being beneficial or dangerous.

It is important to distinguish the difference between evil communication and a mere lack of communication. If someone were to speak to me in Chinese, I would be confused, although the sounds coming from him or her would not necessarily be evil. What would occur in this situation would simply be a lack of meaningful communication that may or may not have serious consequences. In the same way, a trumpet can give a sound that results in confusion, while the sound itself from the trumpet may not necessarily be evil. What has occurred is a lack of meaningful communication.

To determine if the sound from the trumpet were evil, the characteristics of that sound would have to be compared to what Scripture reveals about the characteristics of God. This topic will be addressed more fully in Chapter 5. But for now, the fact that there is a moral aspect to order can be seen as Paul continues his appeal to the Corinthian church. Note that Paul's appeal for understanding continues to include the subject of music: "What is it then? I will pray with the spirit, and I will pray with the understanding also: I will sing with the spirit, and I will sing with the understanding also" (I Corinthians 14:15). (See also I Corinthians 14:26.)

> It is on the basis of the moral aspect of order . . . that Paul appeals for a moral change and a restoration of order in worship.

Paul issues an appeal for meaningful communication and understanding between the members of the Body of Christ: "Brethren, be not children in understanding: howbeit in malice be ye children, but in understanding be men" (I Corinthians 14:20). Now, note that this appeal is based on the nature of God: "For God is not the author of confusion, but of peace, as in all churches of the saints" (I Corinthians 14:33). This is significant. The fact that God is not the author of confusion clearly demonstrates the moral aspect of order. It is on the basis of the moral aspect of order within God's nature that Paul appeals for a moral change and a restoration of order in worship at the Corinthian church.

After reading the Biblical references to "confusion," it is very clear why God is a God of order and not the author of confusion. The first mention of the word *confusion* in the Scriptures is found in Leviticus 18:23: "Neither shalt thou lie with any beast to defile thyself therewith: neither shall any woman stand before a beast to lie down thereto: it is confusion." People are not animals. The seed of humans and the seed of animals do not mix. In God's eyes such a circumstance would result in confusion and therefore is morally forbidden.

Paul writes to the Corinthian church to correct the confusion that was resulting from mixing carnal elements with the spiritual elements of true worship. Likewise, to mix worldly, carnal musical messages with godly, verbal messages is also confusing. The medium communicates a message that may contradict, undermine, or actually change the verbal message. A congregation may remember the emotional, musical messages of a worship service longer than they remember the verbal messages. Therefore, it is of utmost importance to select with care the right music to match the right words—music that supports and confirms God's nature, God's order, and God's Word.

> If God would not sing music that is inconsistent with His nature, who would?

Confirmation that the morality of order applies to the structure of music appears again in Paul's concluding statement: "Let all things be done decently and in order" (I Corinthians 14:40). Does "all things" include music? Yes. Music is indeed included within the category of "all things." God is musical, and there is a design and order to music that is consistent with His nature. It is important to recognize that there is a morality to music itself apart from the lyrics, and what makes music morally right is the way it is arranged to be consistent with God's nature.

If God is not the author of confusion, who is? If God would not sing music that is inconsistent with His nature, who would? Does Satan have a style of music and the power to influence people through that music? He most certainly does.

There is a distinct sound associated with Satan. The language of Isaiah 14:11–12 is so framed as to apply not only to the historical king of Babylon but also to Satan: "Thy pomp is brought down to the grave, and the noise of thy viols [sound; music of thy harps]: the worm is spread under thee, and the worms cover thee. How art thou fallen from heaven, O Lucifer, son of the morning! how art thou cut down to the ground, which didst weaken the nations!" (Isaiah 14:11–12). Note that when Satan fell from heaven and his pomp was brought down to the grave, his musical sound was cast out of heaven with him. When we consider how demonic forces cannot abide in the presence of godly music (see I Samuel 16:14–23), it is clear that Satan has a distinct musical sound that is fundamentally different from the music of God.

The idea that Satan could cunningly pervert God's natural pattern is fully consistent with the teachings of Scripture: "For such are false apostles, deceitful workers, transforming themselves into the apostles of Christ. And no marvel; for Satan himself is transformed into an angel of light. Therefore it is no great thing if his ministers also be transformed as the ministers of righteousness; whose end shall be according to their works" (II Corinthians 11:13–15). Jesus understood the nature of Satan: ". . . He [Satan] was a murderer from the beginning, and abode not in the truth, because there is no truth in him. When he speaketh a lie, he speaketh of his own: for he is a liar, and the father of it" (John 8:44). Peter (see I Peter 5:5) and John (see John 10:10a) also record how Satan uses every means at his disposal to distort and destroy the things God has made for good.

We must be mature in our understanding of music. "Strong meat [instruction for mature believers] belongeth to them that are of full age [mature men and women], even those who by reason of use have their senses exercised to discern both good and evil" (Hebrews 5:14). The word *senses* in this text includes our spiritual sensitivity to moral truth. It includes the physical sense of sight and thus what sights we allow our eyes to see. It also includes the physical sense of hearing and thus what musical sounds we allow our ears to listen to.

The Greek word for *exercised* is *gumnazo* (see #1128), from which we get our word *gymnasium*. We must not, as immature children, carelessly indulge in any kind of musical sound just because we like it or because the lyrics are good. Rather, as mature adults we must "exercise" and discipline ourselves to discern good and evil musical sounds in addition to good and evil musical lyrics.

Our personal preferences of various styles of music are valid only within the bounds of what is morally acceptable to God. Jesus said, "My sheep hear my voice, and I know them, and they follow me" (John 10:27). The purpose of the remainder of this book is to provide an understanding of the nature of the music that is a part of God's being. The only way to gain understanding is to be willing to submit our personal opinions to divine revelation, to honestly follow Jesus in this investigation, and thus conclude with Biblical conviction what is just and holy before the Lord our God and the King of Kings.

Before leaving the topic of order, let's consider two points. The first point is an instance in the Bible where it appeared that God was the author of confusion. The second point involves the moral outworking of order in our lives.

First, on the surface it appears that God was the author of confusion at the Tower of Babel: "Go to, let us go down, and there confound their language, that they may not understand one another's speech" (Genesis 11:7). However, what God created were new phonetic languages, not sounds contrary to His holy nature. The confusion that occurred was the result of human limitations, of which God needed to remind them.

> . . . we must "exercise" and discipline ourselves to discern good and evil musical sounds in addition to good and evil musical lyrics.

Second, many people have not had training that equips them to identify an orderly pattern of music precisely. If music is moral and a note is sung off key, does that imply moral failure on the part of the singer? The answer is obvious if music is considered along with the other qualities God is developing in our lives. Does anyone fully follow the orderly Christlike patterns of love, patience, diligence, self-control, etc.? No. We are all in the process of working out our own salvation with fear and trembling (Philippians 2:12).

Just as we trust God to love others through us to the fullest capacity of our faith, so we trust God to sing through us to the fullest capacity of our faith. We know that we are in a process of maturing in Christ and that we will never be perfect on this earth, so we rest in God's boundless mercies and proceed with reverential fear and trembling, "For it is God which worketh in you . . ." (Philippians 2:13).

There is a significant difference between moving by grace toward a righteous lifestyle and intentionally redefining that lifestyle to align with, or justify, one's personal desires. This is precisely the problem Jesus encountered with the Pharisees, who presented logical reasons to set aside the commandment of God in favor of their personal traditions. However, this was the Lord Jesus Christ's assessment of that reasoning: ". . .Thus have ye made the commandment of God of none effect by your tradition" (Matthew 15:6). We must never transform musical sound that represents a decent and orderly expression of God's nature by altering it in a way that conflicts with His divine likeness, especially if the motive is merely personal preference.

Sound itself carries a message. It may express order according to God's nature, or it may express confusion, which is contrary to God's nature. A musical message that is consistent with God's nature will have orderly characteristics. Its yea will be yea, its nay will be nay, it will be clear, it will communicate a known pattern, it will direct the instruments or singers how to keep the right time as they move through the song together, it will be understood, and it will be conducted decently and in order.

4. AMORAL MUSICAL NOTES FORM MORAL MUSICAL MESSAGES

In our world, in addition to numerous verbal languages, two powerful universal languages exist: art and music. For example, a beautiful landscape painting can communicate the same sense of inspiration to different individuals, independent of their cultures or spoken languages. The same is true of a majestic piece of music.

As explained in IBLP's *Advanced Seminar Textbook*, it is possible to acquire an accurate perception of music by comparing it with principles demonstrated in other methods of communication, both verbal and artistic.[8] By analogy, these same principles may also be observed in other disciplines such as math and chemistry.

Because Thomas Edison applied the universal principles of one discipline (electricity) to other disciplines (chemistry or photography), he developed hundreds of inventions. The laws of these academic disciplines act as an authoritative reference to confirm that musical expression either follows or violates God's principles of design.

The individual components of any language are amoral (i.e., neutral). For example, within verbal languages the individual letters are neutral; within art, individual lines are neutral; within music, individual notes are neutral. In a similar way, the individual components of other disciplines are seen to be neutral. In math individual numbers

> Words are morally right or wrong, and God holds us accountable for them.

are neutral, and in chemistry individual atomic elements (e.g., electrons, protons, and neutrons) are morally neutral.

However, this status of "being neutral" changes when two or more elements are combined. Combinations of two or more letters form words, but combining letters in the wrong way can form idle words. "But I say unto you, That every idle word that men shall speak, they shall give account thereof in the day of judgment. For by thy words thou shalt be justified, and by thy words thou shalt be condemned" (Matthew 12:36–37). The Greek word for *idle* (#692) refers not only to what one might think of as obviously evil, but it also connotes "simply inactive" or "without benefit." The fact that such mild words could be condemned confirms that a level of morality is involved. Individual letters are amoral; however, by our words we shall be justified, or by our words we shall be condemned. Words are morally right or wrong, and God holds us accountable for them.

Likewise, combining lines forms pictures, but combining lines in the wrong way can form pornography, which is morally wrong. Combining notes forms tunes, but combining notes in the wrong way can form musical sounds outside of God's nature and contrary to His design. And by analogy, combining numbers forms equations, but combining numbers in the wrong way can form unbalanced equations and produce a wrong answer. Configuring atomic elements forms compounds, but configuring atomic elements in the wrong way can form poisons, which are potentially damaging to the body.

This law of amoral parts being combined to form a moral result is true in music because it is consistent with other disciplines. These various disciplines serve as a check and balance on each other to verify the accuracy of God's law of design.

Man's Natural Responses

WHY IS IT THAT SOME PEOPLE have never considered the morality of musical sounds? Why is it that others insist that all musical sounds are amoral, that is, neutral or only a matter of personal preference? Following are several possible reasons why some may not be willing to seriously consider the moral aspect of musical sounds.

1. LACK OF VIGILANCE

"Be sober, be vigilant; because your adversary the devil, as a roaring lion, walketh about, seeking whom he may devour" (I Peter 5:8). (See also Ephesians 6:11.) Failure to be vigilant in the area of properly discerning and evaluating musical sounds is an open door for the enemy to introduce immoral sounds that are inconsistent with God's nature, thus perverting true worship, which must be carried out ". . . in spirit and in truth" (John 4:24).

In His Word, God declared these words to His children through Hosea: "My people are destroyed for lack of knowledge: because thou hast rejected knowledge, I will also reject thee . . ." (Hosea 4:6). Many people simply ignore the moral aspects of musical sounds and base their evaluation of the morality of a piece of music strictly on an analysis of its lyrics. While it is important to test the lyrics, the musical sounds themselves must also be tested.

2. CONFUSION AND DECEPTION

Some people have concluded that music is amoral as a result of confusion over the term music. The greatest misunderstanding used to justify worldly music is the often repeated but never supported statement that "music is amoral." This claim is deceptive because it is based on partial truth. Musical notes are indeed amoral, but when they are combined into musical patterns they cease to be amoral and begin to communicate a moral message. Thus, the simple statement that "music is amoral" is both confusing and misleading.

The same tactic of using one term to define two different things is used to promote the deception of evolution. Evolutionary theory claims that there are different types of evolution: cosmic evolution, stellar evolution, human evolution, macroevolution, and microevolution.

Microevolution is actually variation of species, and it is a scientific fact. But obscurity is introduced by renaming variation of species with a new term: microevolution. Then, without solid scientific evidence and a mere association with the term evolution, when microevolution is claimed to be a proof for the other types of evolution, a lie is promoted.

In the same way, there are different types of musical sounds: individual notes and the combination of notes into musical patterns. Individual musical notes themselves are amoral, but without citing any objective Biblical evidence to support their premise, some simply claim that all music is amoral.

In regard to defining terms, Jesus intentionally used the term leaven as an analogy for the disciples in order to help them form an important mental picture. When they misunderstood, note how Jesus interacted with the disciples (e.g., asking them questions) to help them come to a clear understanding of the meaning of that word: "And when his disciples were come to the other side, they had forgotten to take bread. Then Jesus said unto them, Take heed and beware of the *leaven* of the Pharisees and of the Sadducees.

"And they reasoned among themselves, saying, It is because we have taken no bread. Which when Jesus perceived [their confusion and misunderstanding], he said unto them, O ye of little faith, why reason ye among yourselves, because ye have brought no bread? Do ye not yet understand, neither remember the five loaves of the five thousand, and how many baskets ye took up? Neither the seven loaves of the four thousand, and how many baskets ye took up? How is it that ye do not understand that I spake it [bewar e of the leaven] not to you concerning bread, that ye should beware of the leaven of the Pharisees and of the Sadducees?

"Then understood they how that he bade them not beware of the leaven of bread, but of the doctrine of the Pharisees and of the Sadducees" (Matthew 16:5–12).

Jesus was concerned about their "little faith" in viewing life from a subjective cultural experience only, rather than from an objective, divine frame of reference. Jesus wants all of us to identify "leaven" by faith from God's perspective and to understand its meaning in the economy of God's kingdom.

In order to communicate accurately and avoid deception, terms must be defined and understood. Jesus did this by asking questions and by recalling examples and experiences to help the disciples move beyond their subjective cultural experience into an objective understanding of divine truth. The kingdom of God is moving in the direction of faith, and "the just shall live by faith" (Romans 1:17). Like the disciples, we must beware that the leaven of the world is leading in just the opposite direction—away from faith.

> Jesus did not merely clarify the terms . . .

To know the truth about music, we, too, must understand the way musical terms are used (e.g., music, note, beat, rock music, gospel music, Contemporary Christian Music). This knowledge can be achieved by asking questions, by testing statements in the light of Scripture, by providing and requesting documentation, and by sharing the truth with one another in love.

Jesus did not merely clarify the terms, but He also pressed on to provide the disciples with an even deeper understanding of His own divine nature: "When Jesus came into the coasts of Caesarea Philippi, he asked his disciples, saying, Whom do men [in your culture] say that I the Son of man am? And they said, Some say that thou art John the Baptist: some, Elias; and others, Jeremias, or one of the prophets.

"He saith unto them, But whom say ye that I am? And Simon Peter answered and said, Thou art the Christ, the Son of the living God. And Jesus answered and said unto him, Blessed art thou, Simon Barjona: for flesh and blood hath not revealed it unto thee, but my Father which is in heaven" (Matthew 16:13–17). Jesus is asking Peter if he is merely going to agree with what the culture believes about Christ's divine nature. Just as Peter was blessed by the revelation knowledge that Jesus was the Messiah rather than accepting the culture's perception of Jesus, we will be blessed when our beliefs about music are not based on what is widely accepted but rather on what our Heavenly Father reveals to us through His Word.

God is musical. Does the music that you accept clearly reflect His divine nature, or does it reflect merely cultural or personal preference?

3. PRIDE

Some people insist that music is amoral so that they can defend the right to listen to whatever type of musical sound they choose. In contrast to this expression of pride, Scripture exhorts us to prove what is "acceptable unto the Lord" (Ephesians 5:10). Their self-expression is based on subjective experience, in contrast to the divine revelation of Scripture, which is based on objective truth.

The lyrics and musical expressions of today's music increasingly focus on man's personal experience. This trend, the result of an increasing emphasis on the philosophies of humanism and existentialism, which teach gratification of subjective experience as the most desired legitimate expression, will be discussed at length in Chapter 9.

Those who maintain these beliefs tend to reject many traditional Christian hymns on the basis that they are largely doctrinal and because the congregation sings to one another about the Lord in the third person (e.g., "He" is Lord). They prefer to sing contemporary choruses, which often are more personal and which are sung directly to the Lord in the first person (e.g., "You" are Lord).

However, scriptural songs frequently alternate between first- and third-person approaches. (See Exodus 15:1–5, 8–19 in contrast to verses 6–17, Judges 5, and most of the Psalms.) Each "voice" has its proper place, and it is possible to maintain a wholesome focus on the Lord using both the third person and the first person. In both Ephesians 5:19 and Colossians 3:16 we are instructed to be filled with the Spirit, "speaking to yourselves (third person) in psalms and hymns and spiritual songs, singing and making melody in your heart to the Lord (first person)."

The dangerous effect of "leaven" in much of contemporary Christian music occurs when the elements of music communicate a message that exalts subjective experience above objective truth. Scripture warns us that "the flesh lusteth against the Spirit, and the Spirit against the flesh: and these are contrary the one to the other: so that ye cannot do the things that ye would" (Galatians 5:17). If godly words that feed our spirit are mixed with worldly music that feeds our flesh, the result is double-mindedness and instability in all our ways. (See James 1:8.)

Subjective experience is essential, but it must always be tested in the light of objective truth. In books such as *Talking Tombstone & Other Tales of the Media Age* by the secular writer Gary Gumpert, the promoters of "worldly" music insist that "quality is subjective." In other words, they claim that the quality or value of music is entirely subjective to personal preferences. If I like it, if I think it is acceptable and if I am blessed by it, then no one can tell me that it is wrong for me. This is like a drunken man insisting that he is not drunk. His judgment is subjective, but his condition is not; his true condition can be tested objectively by a Breathalyzer.

Our music can and must be tested objectively by the Word of God. If the Bible is the final authority in all matters of life and practice, then we can study it to identify both specific statements and general principles of truth, and we can draw conclusions based on objective revelation—not merely on subjective experience.

The Bible gives an example of someone who thought he was pleasing God when in actuality he was not. Consider Saul's defensive response to Samuel (much like a drunken man) in I Samuel 15:13–22: "And Samuel came to Saul: and Saul said unto him, Blessed be thou of the Lord: I have performed the commandment of the Lord.

> Subjective experience is essential, but it must always be tested in the light of objective truth.

"And Samuel said, What meaneth then this bleating of the sheep in mine ears, and the lowing of the oxen which I hear [obvious objective reality]? And Saul said, They have brought them from the Amalekites: for the people spared the best of the sheep and of the oxen, to sacrifice [i.e. worship—see Psalm 50:13–14] unto the Lord thy God; and the rest we have utterly destroyed.

"Then Samuel said unto Saul, Stay, and I will tell thee what the Lord hath said to me this night. And he said unto him, Say on. And Samuel said, When thou wast little in thine own sight, wast thou not made the head of the tribes of Israel, and the Lord anointed thee king over Israel? And the Lord sent thee on a journey, and said, Go and utterly destroy the sinners the Amalekites, and fight against them until they be consumed. Wherefore then didst thou not obey the voice of the Lord, but didst fly upon the spoil, and didst evil in the sight of the Lord?

"And Saul said unto Samuel, Yea, I have obeyed the voice of the Lord, and have gone the way which the Lord sent me [note the stubborn insistence of self-righteousness], and have brought Agag the king of Amalek, and have utterly destroyed the Amalekites. But the people took of the spoil, sheep and oxen, the chief of the things which should have been utterly destroyed, to sacrifice [worship] unto the Lord thy God in Gilgal.

"And Samuel said, Hath the Lord as great delight in burnt offerings and sacrifices, as in obeying the voice of the Lord? Behold, to obey is better than sacrifice [worship], and to hearken than the fat of rams."

If we bring into worship elements of music that are inconsistent with the nature of God, that is not worship; that is disobedience. It is disobedience because Jesus said, "The hour cometh, and now is, when the true worshippers shall worship the Father in spirit and in truth: for the Father seeketh such to worship him" (John 4:23). The worship of God must be carried out in purity. The very name of the Holy Spirit through Whom we worship the Lord emphasizes this vital point.

The academic disciplines discussed earlier illustrate how adding even a small amount of another element can corrupt an item's purity. Adding a little "white lie" to the truth results in untruth. Adding immodesty to a figure stirs up lust. Adding disorder (in the melody, harmony, or rhythm) to music results in carnal music. Similarly, adding even the value of 1 to a mathematical solution results in an incorrect answer. Adding a small amount of arsenic to water results in poison.

"The holiness of God is no trifling matter. When the nation of Israel lost sight of Who God was and mixed heathen elements into their worship, they brought the judgment of God upon themselves."[1] How much "leaven" does it take to corrupt the whole lump? "Your glorying is not good. Know ye not that a little leaven leaveneth the whole lump?" (I Corinthians 5:6).

If something is morally wrong, such as abortion, and a way is found to justify it (to make it acceptable or morally neutral), as in referring to a baby as a mere fetus or piece of tissue, then individuals are free to decide for themselves about such an act without the fear of anyone (man or God) telling them they are wrong. This freedom to choose what I like, to reserve the right to make the final decision and to act as the final authority in all matters of life and practice, is a prideful expression of humanism. Humanism is a philosophy that denies God and exalts man. It basically states that man can be his own god in every area of this life.

This is the same prideful philosophy that Satan used to deceive Eve when he said to her, "Ye shall be as gods" (Genesis 3:5). If moral absolutes based on Scripture are rejected, man concludes that he is free to do what is right in his own eyes. How sad is the state of man when he decides he can worship God on his own terms. No longer are the Scriptures, the final authority in all matters of life and practice, sought and searched with the goal of gaining wisdom, but rather resolution is sought, through either compromise or force. True freedom is not the license to do what we want but the power to do what we ought—according to Scripture.

4. GREED

"The love of money is the root of all evil" (I Timothy 6:10). The reason that worldly music and much of the Church's CCM is so enormously popular today can be explained simply by the fact that it appeals to the flesh. This issue will be examined further in Chapter 4, but the following quotes support this conclusion:

- "Rock 'n' roll made you want to move and shake and get physically excited." —Janet Podell

- "Rock 'n' roll is musical pornography." —David Noebel in *The Legacy of John Lennon*

Those who promote that style of music know that it sells because it feeds man's lust, self-centeredness, and self-expression.

Jesus rebuked the church at Pergamos because some in their midst held the doctrine of Balaam: "But I have a few things against thee, because thou hast there them that hold the doctrine of Balaam, who taught Balak to cast a stumbling block before the children of Israel, to eat things sacrificed unto idols, and to commit fornication" (Revelation 2:14).

What did Balaam do? As summarized in IBLP's *Advanced Seminar Textbook*: "Balaam was a prophet during the early days of the nation of Israel. He had a special power. Those whom he cursed were cursed, and those whom he blessed were blessed. The King of Moab hired Balaam to curse Israel, but God warned Balaam not to curse His people, so he blessed them instead. However, Balaam's greed and his continued fellowship with God's enemies brought spiritual blindness. His donkey and an angel of God tried to bring Balaam to his senses. He persisted in his own way, got his money, and caused Israel to become morally corrupt."[2]

What "doctrine" is demonstrated by Balaam and his choices? Balaam's doctrine is the leading of God's people astray in the ways of the world for personal gain (e.g. money, popularity, control). Peter referred to this doctrine when he described individuals who ". . . have forsaken the right way, and are gone astray, following the way of Balaam the son of Bosor, who loved the wages of unrighteousness" (II Peter 2:15). Jude also spoke of this error: "Woe unto them! for they have gone in the way of Cain, and ran greedily after the error of Balaam for reward, and perished in the gainsaying of Core" (Jude 1:11).

> Balaam's doctrine is the leading of God's people astray in the ways of the world for personal gain.

CONCLUSION

THERE IS ABUNDANT EVIDENCE, both in Scripture and in the world, regarding the dangers of unclean music. There is no excuse, therefore, for not exercising caution and reexamining the music we allow in our churches, in our homes, and in our lives. Satan is a liar and the father of lies. His greatest lies concerning music are that it is amoral and that we can listen to what we like without any reference to God's truth.

We are in a cultural war. We must fight the good fight of faith. Does the music you set your affections on, aside from its lyrics, represent a worldly lifestyle or a holy way of living? Are you willing to go before God and reevaluate your musical preferences in the light of God's holy nature?

If so, then Section II is intended as a guide to help lead you through the process of searching the Scriptures to discern God's will in regard to the sound of music. The principles presented in Section II represent only a beginning. The Bible is full of principles, testimonies, and truths about this subject.

> There is no excuse, therefore, for not exercising caution and reexamining the music we allow in our churches, in our homes, and in our lives.

However, many of these rich treasures that shed light on the very nature of God are hidden. They await discovery by those who have a hunger and thirst for righteousness: "Yea, if thou criest after knowledge, and liftest up thy voice for understanding; if thou seekest her as silver, and searchest for her as for hid treasures; then shalt thou understand the fear of the Lord, and find the knowledge of God" (Proverbs 2:3–5).

Endnotes: Section I

Chapter 2

1 en.wikipedia.org/wiki/Riot_control and en.wikipedia.org/wiki/Sonic_weapon

2 Kathrine Ames, "An Affair to Remember," Newsweek, October 29, 1990, p. 79

3 www.edu-cyberpg.com/Music/Mice_and_Music_Experiment_Mo.html

4 www.ritholtz.com/blog/2011/02/annualized-cost-of-super-bowl-ad-3-2-tn-german-gdp

5 www.nidcd.nih.gov/health/hearing/noise.asp

6 www.nidcd.nih.gov/health/hearing/pages/noise.aspx

7 www.sightandhearing.org/soundcenter/nihl.asp

8 *Advanced Seminar Textbook*, IBLP, 1986, p. 123

Chapter 3

1 *Advanced Seminar Textbook*, IBLP, 1986, p. 125. See also Psalm 106:34–35 and Isaiah 42:8, 17, 24, and 25.

2 *Advanced Seminar Textbook*, IBLP, 1986, p. 119. See also Numbers chapters 22–24, 31:16.

IN CHAPTER 4 WE WILL IDENTIFY the characteristics of worldly music. These characteristics will stand in stark contrast to the characteristics of godly music. In Chapter 5 we will examine the specific characteristics of melody, harmony, and rhythm that compose godly music when they are balanced and worldly music when they are unbalanced. Then in Chapter 6 we will learn the danger of mixing that which is unclean and worldly with that which is clean and holy.

A Prayer for God's Perspective

". . . Our Father which art in heaven, Hallowed be thy name. Thy kingdom come. Thy will be done in earth, as it is in heaven" (Matthew 6:9–10).

Chapter 4

Discerning Worldly Music

BEFORE LISTING THE CHARACTERISTICS of worldly music, it will be instructive to hear the world's evaluation of its own music. God wants believers to be a wise and understanding people: "Behold, I have taught you statutes and judgments, even as the Lord my God commanded me, that ye should do so in the land whither ye go to possess it. Keep therefore and do them; for this is your wisdom and your understanding in the sight of the nations, which shall hear all these statutes, and say, Surely this great nation is a wise and understanding people. For what nation is there so great, who hath God so nigh unto them, as the Lord our God is in all things that we call upon him for?" (Deuteronomy 4:5–7).

Regarding victorious Christian living in the areas of marriage oneness, family harmony, health, and finances, are believers a wise and understanding people today? The United States of America became great because our Founding Fathers understood the greatness of Biblical truth and how to apply it to life. The United States is losing its greatness because Americans have lost sight of the greatness of the statutes and commandments of the God of our fathers and are failing to apply them to every area of our lives, including the area of music.

Many people are testing the words of music, but few are applying Biblical principles to test the musical sound itself. This is dangerous because of music's prominent place in society and its powerful influence as a universal language. The Bible warns about the danger of a lack of knowledge: "My people are destroyed for lack of knowledge: because thou hast rejected knowledge, I will also reject thee, that thou shalt be no priest to me: seeing thou hast forgotten the law of thy God, I will also forget thy children" (Hosea 4:6).

Jesus confirms this warning: "And the lord commended the unjust steward, because he had done wisely: for the children of this world are in their generation wiser than the children of light" (Luke 16:8). Given what the children of this world are saying about their own ungodly music, it is unbelievable to observe what the children of light are allowing to enter the church, unexamined and untested. As we look at what the world says about its own unclean music, we will see how opposed it is to God's holy law.

> . . . for the children of this world are in their generation wiser than the children of light.

First consider the power of music to influence not only an individual life but also an entire culture.

- The *Shu Ching*, or *Book of History* (sixth century B.C.), is the oldest complete work among what are known as the five Confucian classics. It states, "For changing people's manners and altering their customs there is nothing better than music."[1] According to this observation, musical sound that is not consistent with God's nature and character would have the power to alter godly customs and the Christian way of life.

- Confucius (500 B.C.) said, "If you would know if a people are well-governed [self-controlled], and if its laws are good or bad, examine the music it practices."[2] According to this observation, a well-governed people will be characterized by well-governed music. If you were to examine your music in the light of Biblical truth, what would you find?

- In his work *Politics*, Aristotle (340 B.C.) wrote, "Music directly imitates the passions or states of the soul; . . . when one listens to music that imitates certain passion, he becomes imbued with the same passion; and if over a long time he habitually listens to the kind of music that rouses ignoble passions his whole character will be shaped to an ignoble form."[3] Note that Aristotle understood how music entailed far more than words. As the language of emotion it has the power to shape the character.

- The Roman philosopher Boethius (500 A.D.) stated, "Music is a part of us, and either ennobles or degrades our behavior."[4] According to this observation, music is not neutral (amoral); it either ennobles or degrades. As Jesus pointed out, this worldly philosopher may well be wiser than many children of light.

- Plato said: "Through foolishness they deceived themselves into thinking that there was no right or wrong in music—that it was to be judged good or bad by the pleasure it gave. By their work and their theories they infected the masses with the presumption to think themselves adequate judges."[5] This is recognition of the age-old tactic of rejecting absolute truth in a certain area of life in order to justify a personal, subjective preference. Pride is reserving for ourselves the right to make the final decision about what is right or wrong.

Consider also the ungodly nature of much of the popular worldly music as confessed by "the children of this world" in these more recent statements.

- The article on "rock and roll" in Wikipedia defines the origin of the phrase *rock and roll*. It states that the word *rock* had a long history in the English language as a metaphor for "to shake up, to disturb, or to incite." The idea is to shake someone up, to disturb his rest, to intimidate him, or to incite to rebellion. The term *rock* describes the violence and rebellion associated with that style of music. The verb *roll* was a medieval metaphor that meant "having sex." Writers for hundreds of years have used the phrases "they had a roll in the hay" or "I rolled her in the clover." Note the association of wrath (rock) with fornication (roll) in Scripture: "For all nations have drunk of the wine of the wrath [rock] of her fornication [roll]" (Revelation 18:3, 8).

- "Rock can't be made respectable. . . . The music will simply subvert the words. . . . No matter how many reforms are attempted, rock and rap will always gravitate in the direction of violence [rock] and uncommitted sex [roll]. The beat says, 'Do what you want to do.' "[6]

- "Rock is all there is. . . . The words make little difference; they may be explicitly sexual, or sermons in favor of nuclear disarmament, or even religious—the motor of it all is eroticism."[7]

- "Rock 'n' roll is musical pornography."[8]

- "All rock is revolutionary. By its very beat and sound it has always implicitly rejected restraints and has celebrated freedom and sexuality."[9] Notice that the use of the word *freedom* here is inaccurate. This kind of freedom is only the perceived freedom associated with the rejection of moral restraints. A more appropriate term in the context of rejecting restraints would be *rebellion*. This perceived freedom is actually slavery, as Jesus stated: "Jesus answered them, Verily, verily, I say unto you, Whosoever committeth sin [rejection of moral restraint] is the servant of sin" (John 8:34). Thus, what this quote is actually recognizing is that rock music is a celebration of rebellion and sexual immorality that will enslave those caught up in it. (See also II Peter 2:18–19.)

- Quote from a surviving Branch Davidian Cult member: "He controlled us with rock music."[10]

- Rock music was used in Russia to torment believers.[11]

- "There is more blatant immorality being peddled in popular music now than ever before"[12] Yes, music, as well as all other matters of life and practice, must be reconsidered in the light of Scripture if it is to be acceptable to God.

- Bob Dylan, a song writer and musician whose works date from the 1960s, told an interviewer, "If I told you what our music is really about, we'd probably all get arrested."[13]

What elements in music would make it ungodly, would cause a song writer to be concerned about getting arrested, or would torment Russian believers?

Wikipedia identifies some of the elements of rock and roll by stating that the beat is essentially a blues rhythm with an accentuated back-beat, which is almost always provided by a snare drum. Classic rock and roll is usually played with one or two electric guitars (one lead, one rhythm), a string bass or (after the mid-1950s) an electric bass guitar, and a drum kit.

Based on this description, a key element of music that needs to be evaluated is the *beat*. This is confirmed by the following statement: "When pulsation and syncopation are the rhythmic foundations of the music the movements of the dancers can invariably be seen to become very sensual."[14] Thus, the rhythm contains the primary elements in music that can accentuate sensuality, cause a song writer to be concerned about its legality, and torment Russian believers.

Although there is a difference between the beat and the rhythm, the two terms are often used interchangeably. The difference between these two terms as used in this book will be explained in Chapter 5. But for now, simply consider the beat as equal units of time where a tone may or may not be sounded on each beat. The rhythm, on the other hand, is created by the tones that are sounded. Thus, a key element of worldly music that needs to be evaluated is the rhythm.

The children of this world are describing the characteristics of their own music. The elements of melody, harmony, and especially rhythm are being intentionally manipulated in order to communicate a message and lifestyle that are contrary to God's nature and God's law.

The primary characteristics of most contemporary music in the United States today, either secular or religious, are (1) a dominant rhythm, (2) excessive repetition, and (3) high tension. The dominant rhythm is loud, prevailing over the melody and harmony. It is often referred to as a "dominant beat" and is usually accompanied with syncopation, highly accented back-beats, break-beats, and poly-rhythms. Excessive repetition may occur in a melodic phrase, a harmonic pattern, a rhythmic pattern, or any combination of these. High tension is a combination of musical elements that include fast tempo, loud volume, excessive dissonance in the harmony, and excessive variation in the rhythm.

> The elements of melody, harmony, and especially rhythm are being intentionally manipulated in order to communicate a message and lifestyle that are contrary to God's nature and God's law.

Let's contrast the characteristics of these three musical elements with the characteristics of Biblical Christlike living.

1. HOW A DOMINANT RHYTHM CAN STIR UP REBELLION

God has a master design and purpose for His creation. This purpose was foreordained before the foundation of the world.

(See I Peter 1:19.) This plan of redemption includes common elements needed by all men yet allows unique experiences for different individuals. Thus, there is a supreme theme to God's design that allows for variations of that theme.

For example, some of the basic elements of God's plan of redemption include the virgin birth of Christ as the spotless Lamb of God, the death of Christ as our substitute, the burial of Christ, the resurrection of Christ, and the return of Christ: "For I delivered unto you first of all that which I also received, how that Christ died for our sins according to the scriptures; and that he was buried, and that he rose again the third day according to the scriptures" (1 Corinthians 15:3–4). One individual may have a special need for mercy offered by the works of Christ and thus experience a special sense of forgiveness. (See Luke 7:47.) Another person may have a special need for meaning and purpose offered by the works of Christ and thus experience a special sense of fulfillment. (See Acts 9:6.) Another way of recognizing this variation is to note the various ways the Holy Spirit brings personal conviction. "And when he is come, he will reprove the world of sin, and of righteousness, and of judgment" (John 16:8).

The revelation of God's theme and order has a definite beginning (confirming creation, the origin of man, the origin of sin, etc.), builds to a climax (highlighting redemption through the crucifixion and resurrection of Christ), and culminates with a definite sense of conclusion (promising rest in the blessed hope of Christ's final return to reward and to judge). While there are variations of this theme, God has established this order as an expression of His character and His will in heaven and on earth.

Therefore, a musical form that follows this order communicates a godly message that leaves the listener satisfied that a "statement" has been made [a beginning], the intention of the statement understood [a climax], and the piece completed [a conclusion]. On the other hand, a musical form that distorts or omits this order communicates an ungodly message of distraction and rejection.

Consider two familiar songs and how the climax portion of each song communicates God's order. Begin by singing out loud the musical form of the chorus of the song "Jesus Loves Me" and note how the music builds to a climax and then concludes as follows: "Yes, Jesus loves me [beginning]. Yes, Jesus loves me [repetition]. Yes, Jesus loves me [climax]. The Bible tells me

> Music that is characterized by a dominant rhythm throughout overpowers the sense of a climax.

so [conclusion]." The aspect of God's divine plan of redemption that is spoken of in this song is that Jesus loves me. And the climax in the musical form enforces this statement in the lyrics.

Another example can be seen in the chorus of the song "It Is Well With My Soul," which reaches a climax and concludes as follows: "It is well, with my soul [beginning]. It is well. It is well [climax], with my soul [conclusion]." In both of these examples there is a beginning that builds to an obvious climax and reaches a definite sense of conclusion according to God's order and design.

However, music that is characterized by a dominant rhythm throughout overpowers the sense of a climax. The variation on the theme is so dominant that it cancels out the melodic theme. The message in such a musical form is inconsistent with God's design and order. The emotional message of this style of music is one that overpowers and cancels out the climax, not only issuing a challenge to, but also actually rejecting and rebelling against, the crowning work of the Savior.

The lyrics of the song may acknowledge the Savior, but the musical form of the song proclaims a deeper emotional message that denies Him. And without a Savior, every man is *free* from the restraint of rules so that he can do what is right in his own eyes. And this is exactly what was observed, as noted above by William Kilpatrick, who stated, "The beat says 'Do what you want to do.'"

> The lyrics of the song may acknowledge the Savior, but the musical form of the song proclaims a deeper emotional message that denies Him.

The Bible gives a strong warning to those who leave God and His ways out of their lives: "The wicked shall be turned into hell, and all the nations that forget God" (Psalm 9:17). We must never forget God, whether it is in daily conversations, business decisions, finances, scheduling, art, or any other area of life, including musical lyrics and musical forms.

At first the worldly rhythm often enters a life or a church in a mild form, like a little leaven of which we are admonished to be aware. The musical message in the melody, harmony, and words is only slightly blurred and confused by an unnatural rhythm. Like a frog sitting in a pot of water that is slowly brought to a boil, the danger of the unnatural rhythms is gradually accepted.

Scripture speaks of the song of fools: "It is better to hear the rebuke of the wise, than for a man to hear the song of fools" (Ecclesiastes 7:5). The contrast here is between wisdom and foolishness, between that which is of God and that which is vain, empty, and hollow (i.e., without godly order and purpose).

"Foolishness is bound in the heart of a child [one who is unaware of consequences, without knowledge]; but the rod of correction shall drive it far from him" (Proverbs 22:15). Recall the statement from the *Book of History*: "For changing people's manners and altering their customs there is nothing better than music." How much more, then, can foolish music reinforce the foolishness that is already bound in the heart. That is why it does not take a lot of the dominant rhythm or syncopation to cause children to become silly and foolish in their behavior. The same can be observed in adults who lack godly wisdom, as evidenced by their actions in dances such as the jitter bug or the twist.

Vain philosophies leave God out and justify their actions with excuses such as "everyone is doing it" or "it is cute." "Beware lest any man spoil you through philosophy and vain deceit, after the tradition of men, after the rudiments of the world, and not after Christ" (Colossians 2:8).

But sinful, self-centered behavior satisfies only for a season (see Hebrews 11:25), with the consequence of stirring up even greater lusts. This progression of sin is explained by the phrase "gave them up" three times in Romans 1:21–32. After a time, the worldly rhythm progressively increases to the point of making the godly musical message in the melody, harmony, and words less and less noticeable.

Finally, the orderly musical message in the melody, harmony, and words is swallowed up by the controlling rhythm. The strong rhythm eventually becomes the primary theme as well as the desire of the listener.

The emotional message in such a theme is that of another gospel: God is dead and the ultimate expression is self-expression. More about these false gospels of tribal worship and neo-orthodoxy will be explained in Section III. The Bible gives a warning to those who justify such a message: "Woe unto them that call evil good, and good evil; that put darkness for light, and light for darkness; that put bitter for sweet, and sweet for bitter!" (Isaiah 5:20).

2. HOW EXCESSIVE REPETITION CAN STIR UP SENSUALITY

Section III will provide a historical overview of unclean music, but for now we will observe how the repetitive rhythm of the drum was used in Biblical times to drown out the voice of the conscience and stir up perverted behavior. Solomon's wives turned away his heart after other gods: "For it came to pass, when Solomon was old, that his wives turned away his heart after other gods: and his heart was not perfect with the LORD his God, as was the heart of David his father" (I Kings 11:4). He built them beautiful high places for their worship: "And the high places that were before Jerusalem, which were on the right hand of the mount of corruption, which Solomon the king of Israel had builded for Ashtoreth the abomination of the Zidonians, and for Chemosh the abomination of the Moabites, and for Milcom the abomination of the children of Ammon . . ." (II Kings 23:13).

The hill on which these high places were built is still known as the Mount of Corruption. This part of Olivet was called the high place of Tophet: "And they have built the high places of Tophet, which is in the valley of the son of Hinnom, to burn their sons and their daughters in the fire; which I commanded them not, neither came it into my heart" (Jeremiah 7:31). This is confirmed by Josiah, who later destroyed Topheth as part of his great religious reforms: "And he defiled Topheth, which is in the valley

> The repetitive rhythm of the drum was used in Biblical times to drown out the voice of the conscience and stir up perverted behavior.

of the children of Hinnom, that no man might make his son or his daughter to pass through the fire to Molech" (II Kings 23:10).

After these high places were destroyed, the "valley of the children of Hinnom" became a reference for hell. The word *hell* in the New Testament is *geenna* [#1067], which means "valley of [the son of] Hinnom." Based on what is known of Solomon's other elaborate works, the high places he made for his wives must have been beautiful gardens—sin was made to look very appealing. So today, pornography, divorce, abortion, sodomy, worldly music, and other perversions are all made to look attractive and acceptable. God judged Solomon's sinful practices and turned these beautiful gardens into a place for burning garbage.

It has been discovered that this high place was also called the Garden of Tophet or the Garden of the Drum because the people were led into a drug-like trance through the driving rhythm of the drums as they sacrificed their children. This is consistent with the definition of *Tophet* in Webster's

1828 Dictionary, an Early American dictionary that defines terms using references to Scripture. It states the following: [Hebrew: tophet, a drum.] "Hell; so called from a place east of Jerusalem where children were burnt to Moloch, and where drums were used to drown their cries."

> ... the people were led into a drug-like trance through the driving rhythm of the drums as they sacrificed their children.

The hypnotic effect of excessive repetition dulls the senses, lowers restraint and self-control, and promotes rebellion against the conscience, all contributing to perverted behavior. Note that we cannot judge the sincerity of the worshippers at these high places of pagan worship. To be willing to sacrifice their children they must have been very sincere and serious about their worship. However, we must, in harmony with God's truth, condemn their immoral practices.

The unthinkable act of sacrificing a child in worship should sound a serious alarm to the danger of the dulling of the senses by the power of repetition. Repeating an action over and over again can build a bad habit and harden the heart, whether it is consciously realized or not. Excessive repetition, careless familiarity, lowering one's guard, complacency, and compromise are all too familiar tendencies of the sinful human nature.

> Sin is a monster of such awful mein
> that to be hated needs but to be seen
> but seen to oft familiar of face
> we first endure, then pity, then embrace.
> —Alexander Pope

3. HOW HIGH TENSION
CAN "SOW TO THE FLESH"

The music of the world can be described as intense. One element of music is tempo. Tempo is the speed of music, which can change at various times in a song. The number of beats per measure is specified by the time signature, but how long each beat is held, which determines the tempo, is specified by the composer, conductor, pianist, or song leader. Once the tempo is set, it remains the same, providing order, unless it is intentionally changed, providing variation.

If the tempo is fast it creates a sensation of tension (i.e. excitement, urgency), but if it is too fast the music exhausts the listener and creates a sensation of excessiveness or wildness, like a stampede. Music that is too fast communicates a musical message that violates the Biblical principle that we should not run ahead of God. "Also, that the soul be without knowledge, it is not good; and he that hasteth with his feet sinneth" (Proverbs 19:2).

If the tempo is slow it creates a sensation of relaxation (i.e., a quiet, meditative mood), but if it is too slow the music drags and creates a sensation of boredom and apathy. Music that is too slow communicates a musical message that violates the Biblical principle of not lagging behind God in slothfulness. "Then he said unto them, O fools, and slow of heart to believe all that the prophets have spoken" (Luke 24:25). "Not slothful in business; fervent in spirit; serving the Lord" (Romans 12:11). If the music is orderly it helps one sing with God in harmony with His design; if it is disorderly it leads one to sing on his own, apart from God and His ways.

Tension is the sensation of being stretched or tested. The opposite of tension is the sensation of being relaxed or re-solved. There is a proper place for both tension and relaxation in God's nature, in life, and in music.

The elements of tension in music include high tones (i.e., frequencies), rhythm, dissonance (i.e. clashing in the harmony), and loud volume. The elements of relaxation in music include low tones, melody, consonance (i.e., blending in the harmony), and soft volume.

High tension occurs as the stretching reaches the point of stress, confusion, alarm, or danger. Most contemporary music is made up almost entirely of high tension.

This high tension in worldly music reinforces the rejec-tion of restraints in the flesh and communicates a message of disorder. When there was an absence of law and order on our western frontier, the West became known as the "wild West."

The rejection of law and order became popular in the 1960s, and that rebellion was promoted through educational philoso-phies, art, and music. Is it any wonder that our culture has become so "wild," with less and less self-control and greater and greater degrees of immorality and violence?

High tension in the music both reflects and reinforces the wild nature of the flesh: "For he that soweth to his flesh shall of the flesh reap corruption; but he that soweth to the Spirit shall of the Spirit reap life everlasting" (Galatians 6:8).

In the book *Solomon's Secret*, Ray Stedman explains King Solomon's observation about man's search for the secret of happiness and contentment: "After we have sucked dry all the immediate delight, joy, or pleasure of something, what is left over, what endures, what will remain to continually feed the hunger of our lives for satisfaction?"[15]

The flesh looks for lasting enjoyment in things, pleasures, relationships, religion, or music, but none of these has enduring value in and of itself. Many have seized onto high-tension music and are trying to make it satisfy, but as Solomon discovered, there is nothing in man, no inherent value in the natural man, that makes it possible for him to extract true enjoyment from the things he does. There is no stimulant, no being "drunk with wine," no being "high on drugs," no "high tension in music" that satisfies.

True satisfaction is a gift of God. (See Ecclesiastes 2:24–26a.) Man receives this gift by sowing to the Spirit (see Galatians 6:8), by letting the Word of Christ dwell in him richly in all wisdom, and the result, the joyous gift of God, is ". . . teaching and admonishing one another in psalms and hymns and spiritual songs." (See Colossians 3:16.)

> There is no stimulant, no being "drunk with wine," no being "high on drugs," no "high tension in music" that satisfies.

Sowing to the flesh puts the cart before the horse. Instead of using music as a spiritual drug to stimulate an emotional experience, God instructs us first to be filled with the Spirit, and then the result will be singing and making melody in your heart to the Lord. (See Ephesians 5:18–19.) God will actually be singing His song through us, just like He loves through us, gives through us, and works through us!

Orderly music has a mixture of tension and relaxation. There are times when the music builds to a climax, and then there are other times when it relaxes. All orderly music is patterned after God's nature, with a balance between tension and relaxation. In orderly music, the elements of tension are always under strict control.

High tension is to music as salt is to a meal. It would not be healthy or appetizing to eat a meal that was 99% salt or 50% salt or even 10% salt. In the same way, music with high tension is out of balance and sows to the flesh. The tension needs to be under strict control.

In light of what the world is saying about its own music and in light of the fact that worldly music is not consistent with the nature of God, the following warnings should be taken seriously:

- "Be not conformed to this world . . ." (Romans 12:2).

- "Know ye not that the friendship of the world is enmity with God?" (James 4:4).

- "Love not the world, neither the things that are in the world. If any man love the world, the love of the Father is not in him" (I John 2:15).

The "world" in this context refers to the system of thinking or singing that is contrary to God's way of thinking or singing, leading to actions, attitudes, and appearances contrary to the believer's walk as taught in Scripture.

CHAPTER **5**

Discerning Godly Music

HOW DO WE DISCERN TRUTH? Truth is revealed objectively by the divine revelation of the Word: "And the Word was made flesh, and dwelt among us, (and we beheld his glory, the glory as of the only begotten of the Father,) full of grace and truth" (John 1:14).

Truth is discerned with our spiritual nature rather than just with our human nature: "But the natural man receiveth not the things of the Spirit of God: for they are foolishness unto him: neither can he know them, because they are spiritually discerned" (I Corinthians 2:14). This means that truth is discerned objectively as our spirit listens to God's Word, not subjectively as we listen to the thoughts of our own mind or the feelings of our own emotions.

"For the word of God is quick, and powerful, and sharper than any two-edged sword, piercing even to the dividing asunder of soul and spirit, and of the joints and marrow, and is a discerner of the thoughts and intents of the heart" (Hebrews 4:12). Thus, we are not looking for a mere intellectual set of rules about music or an emotionally acceptable set of sounds. Truth is discerned in our spirit by applying Scriptural principles, not just by evaluation with our mind and our emotions. Therefore, in this chapter the approach to discern godly music will be to describe the basic parts of musical sound, examine the nature and behavior of each part, and then compare them with the nature and behavior of God as revealed in the Bible.

There is a wide variety of ways that musical notes can be combined to form the three basic parts of music: melody, harmony, and rhythm. The manner in which these notes are combined has consequences. Together they form the powerful language of music that has significant effect apart from the lyrics.

As with all other aspects of God's physical creation, melody, harmony, and rhythm were designed to reflect truth about God's nature (what He is like and the kind of Person He is) and about God's will (what He is doing and the way He works): "For the invisible things of him from the creation of the world are clearly seen, being understood by the things that are made, even his eternal power and Godhead; so that they are without excuse" (Romans 1:20). Clearly, the spiritual nature of God can be understood in terms of the physical things He has made. Thus, it is possible to examine the physical things God has created and understand something of His divine nature. For example: "Go to the ant, thou sluggard; consider her ways, and be wise" (Proverbs 6:6). When God designed the ant He instilled in the ant's behavior certain qualities like His divine nature.

> Truth is discerned objectively as our spirit listens to God's Word, not subjectively as we listen to the thoughts of our own mind or the feelings of our own emotions.

By studying the ant's ways we can gain wisdom and learn what God is like. Of course, the nature of God revealed in the things He has made will never contradict the nature of God revealed in Scripture. Only those aspects of creation, including music, that are consistent with the character and nature of God will be fit instruments in His hand to further His will being done on earth as it is in heaven.

Have you ever examined how musical sound itself, apart from the lyrics, is or is not consistent with the Biblical revelation about the nature of God? Would you be willing to test the spirit of your music and prove whether it is acceptable unto the Lord? (See Ephesians 5:10.) Are you willing to allow God to change you and your music more and more into His image? "But we all, with open face beholding as in a glass the glory of the Lord, are changed into the same image from glory to glory, even as by the Spirit of the Lord" (II Corinthians 3:18).

> The spiritual nature of God can be understood in terms of the physical things He has made.

1. MELODY

Melody is typically the part of music that we hum. We perceive sounds as being relatively high or low. This property is called pitch or tone. By definition, melody is made up of a series of rising and falling pitches. To put it simply, the melody is the part of music that rises and falls.

The only New Testament word translated as *melody* is *psallo* [#5667], which means "to touch the surface; to play on a stringed instrument; to make melody, or to sing (psalms)."

"And be not drunk with wine, wherein is excess; but be filled with the Spirit; speaking to yourselves in psalms and hymns and spiritual songs, singing and making melody in your heart to the Lord" (Ephesians 5:18–19).

The Greek word *psallo* is most often translated as the word *sing*, which fundamentally includes melody. For example, a soloist cannot sing harmony because there is nothing for his single voice to harmonize with. So when David sang psalms by himself out in the fields with his sheep, he sang melody. When he picked up his harp, however, he could harmonize with his instrument as he sang the melody. The fact that melody is a fundamental component of singing is evident when we consider how a line of harmony can become a melody all its own when it is sung by itself.

The most common way to observe the relationship between singing and melody is to listen to how people sing a familiar song. Unless they are trained in music they will most likely sing that song in their natural range, and what they will be singing is the melody line.

The point is that the melody, not necessarily the harmony, is what is always sung. Therefore, it is understandable why *psallo* is translated as *melody* or *singing*, not excluding the presence of harmony and rhythm, but predominantly including the melody of the song. Thus, *psallo* is an appropriate New Testament word for *melody*.

Melodies do not just happen. Rather, they are specifically designed to move in certain ways. A composer arranges a few pitches to make a short melodic formula called a motive.

In the song "Jesus Loves Me," the verses are composed of four motives, where the third motive is a repeat of the first motive. "Jesus loves me; this I know" is motive A; "For the Bible tells me so" is a different motive B; "Little ones to Him belong" repeats melodic formula A; and "They are weak, but He is strong" is a new motive C. Thus we see how melodies are made up of motives.

Recall from Chapter 1 how there exists a spiritual sound of music in the heart of God that can take on a physical dimension in the physical world. And according to Romans 1:20 the physical things that are made (such as musical sounds) can help us clearly see the invisible things of God (His musical nature). Therefore, an analysis of the physical parts of musical sound can help us understand something of the spiritual song that is in the heart of God. Of course, Scripture must confirm any parallel that is observed between the physical characteristics of music and the spiritual nature of God. Nevertheless, the fact remains that one can begin with an analysis of the physical characteristics of music and understand something of the equivalent spiritual nature of God. Thus, we have a basis for examining a piece of music, comparing its characteristics with the attributes of

> An analysis of the physical parts of musical sound can help us understand something of the spiritual song that is in the heart of God.

God, and concluding with an objective evaluation of its morality. Isn't this just the criteria that we use to discern godliness in other areas? Consider how we evaluate a spiritual leader's qualifications. We examine his character in light of what we know about God's character, and if a question arises about a specific quality, then we form a conclusion using Scripture as our final authority.

Melody is the first of the three parts of music that we will examine to understand the musical nature of God and His moral will. Because God is a God of order, physical melodies must be balanced in their design of rising and falling pitches in order to accurately reflect the spiritual melodies in the heart of God. Let's look at how balance or imbalance in their rise and fall communicates a message that is consistent or inconsistent with God's nature and His will.

Rising Melody

Rising melody lines build a natural tension through a sense of expectation and excitement. A rise in melody builds a normal sense of tension, just as some tension is a natural part of life.

Because a spiritual melody exists in the heart of God, a spiritual rise with a divine tension and expectation also exists in His heart. In music, the opposite of relaxation is tension. In life the opposite of lying down (relaxation) is rising up (tension), which reflects the eagerness, anticipation, and excitement of a new day. Numerous times in the book of Jeremiah God describes Himself as rising up early: "And now, because ye have done all these works, saith the LORD, and I spake unto you, rising up early and speaking, but ye heard not; and I called you, but ye answered not" (Jeremiah 7:13). David pleaded for God to arise with a normal sense of tension to take action: "Let God arise, let his enemies be scattered . . ." (Psalm 68:1). "Arise, O God, plead thine own cause . . ." (Psalm 74:22). When Jesus saw human needs, He often responded with a normal sense of tension and was moved to action: "And Jesus went forth, and saw a great multitude, and was moved with compassion toward them, and he healed their sick" (Matthew 14:14).

However, excessive rising in the melody before any downward turn builds high tension and creates a sense of dissatisfaction. Frustration arises in the listener because the rise is not resolved, the expectation is not fulfilled, and the promise is not kept.

Excessive rising in the melody is not a common occurrence, but when it occurs does it accurately represent the melody that is in the heart of God? To answer this question, consider the characteristic of excessive rising in the melody and compare that characteristic with the character of God. Excessive rising in the melody expresses expectation without resolution. Is it characteristic of God to stir up expectations without fulfillment of those expectations or promises? No. One aspect of God's nature is His faithfulness. While He may wait for a time, He can be counted on to fulfill and resolve all His promises! "For all the promises of God in him are yea, and in him Amen, unto the glory of God by us" (II Corinthians 1:20). Therefore, excessive rising in the melody cannot be consistent with God's nature. Excessive rising in the melody communicates a musical message that God is unfaithful.

> Excessive rising in the melody communicates a musical message that God is unfaithful.

We all know what it is like to have an issue arise, to be attempting to solve it, and to experience the frustration of not being able to reach a resolution. Now imagine all the unresolved moral issues in the world. Are frustration and anxiety in the heart of God as He actively works to bring about His solutions? No. Another aspect of God's nature is His peace. He is at peace as He works to bring about His will on earth. Ultimately, we may be assured that "the God of peace shall bruise Satan under your feet shortly . . ." (Romans 16:20). Again, the excessive tension created by the excessive rising in the melody is not consistent with this aspect of God's nature. Excessive rising in the melody communicates a musical message that God is not a God of peace.

Is it God's will for us to live with excessive tension? No. Neither should the message in the melodies we choose to listen to create excessive tension. What Biblical truth would be violated by the imbalance of excessive rising in the melody? "Be careful [anxious] for nothing; but in every thing by prayer and supplication with thanksgiving let your requests be made known unto God" (Philippians 4:6).

The message in the melody should not lead the listener into anxiety, which is contrary to God's will: "And the peace of God, which passeth all understanding, shall keep your hearts and minds through Christ Jesus" (Philippians 4:7). If we want God's peace to rule in our hearts, then we should make choices, including music choices, that are consistent with the way God works to impart His peace: "And let the peace of God rule in your hearts, to the which also ye are called in one body; and be ye thankful" (Colossians 3:15).

Falling Melody

Falling melody lines create a natural relaxation through a sense of calmness or resolution, as can be observed in watching falling leaves or falling snow. A fall in melody creates a normal sense of relaxation, just as some relaxation is a natural part of life.

Because a spiritual melody exists in the heart of God, the spiritual *fall* of a divine relaxation and calmness also exists in His heart. The Bible speaks of God resting in His love, a rest that is like the calm, silent joy in possessing a love too great for words to express. (See Zephaniah 3:17.) This is just what God did after the six days of creation when He rested with a quiet satisfaction in His work, for "behold, it was very good." (See Genesis 2:2, 1:31.)

> Excessive descending in the melody before any upward turn induces excessive relaxation and creates a sense of defeat.

However, excessive descending in the melody before any upward turn induces excessive relaxation and creates a sense of defeat. Despair depresses the listener because the fall is not recovered, the answer is not given, and the hope is not offered.

Excessive falling in the melody would be associated with much of the doom and oppression in musical styles such as death metal, but does this accurately represent the melody that is in the heart of God? To answer this question, consider the characteristic of excessive falling in the melody and compare that characteristic with the character of God. Excessive falling in the melody expresses failure without recovery. Is it characteristic of God to have no answers for the failures and problems in the world? No. One aspect of God's nature is that He is the Savior of the world: "For God sent not his Son into the world to condemn the world; but that the world through him might be saved" (John 3:17). His chief purpose for entering the human race is to save us from our sins: "And she shall bring forth a son, and thou shalt call his name JESUS: for he shall save his people from their sins" (Matthew 1:21). Therefore, excessive falling in the melody cannot be consistent with God's nature. Excessive falling in the melody communicates a musical message that God does not have a solution for sin and death.

We all know what it is like to get discouraged and "be down". Now imagine all the moral failures in the world. Are despair and hopelessness in the heart of God as He patiently works to draw mankind to Himself? No. Another aspect of God's nature is that He is our hope: "Paul, an apostle of Jesus Christ by the commandment of God our Savior, and Lord Jesus Christ, which is our hope" (I Timothy 1:1). Again, the excessive relaxation created by the excessive falling in the melody is not consistent with this aspect of God's nature. Excessive falling in the melody communicates a musical message that God is not a God of hope. Because Jesus Christ is our hope, a melody that does not ultimately communicate hope is actually a denial of Christ. The musical message communicated by excessive falling in the melody proclaims the false doctrine that there is no hope in the risen Lord Jesus Christ.

> Excessive falling in the melody communicates a musical message that God is not a God of hope.

Is it God's will for us to live with excessive relaxation? No. Neither should the message in the melody line reflect excessive relaxation. What Biblical truth would be violated by the perversion of excessive falling in the melody? "For a just man falleth seven times, and riseth up again: but the wicked shall fall into mischief" (Proverbs 24:16). It is not God's desire to leave a just man in a fallen state: "The steps of a good man are ordered [#3559] by the Lord: and he delighteth in his way. Though he fall, he shall not be utterly cast down: for the Lord upholdeth him with his hand" (Psalm 37:23–24). God arranges the steps of a good man by principles of order and design. Therefore, the message in the melody should not leave the listener with a sense of being utterly cast down, and it should not lead the listener into hopelessness contrary to God's will. The Biblical doctrine that is denied by this imbalance in the melody is the doctrine of our blessed hope: "Why art thou cast down, O my soul? and why art thou disquieted in me? hope thou in God: for I shall yet praise him for the help of his countenance" (Psalm 42:5). If we desire to live with a blessed hope in our heart, then we should make choices, including music choices, which are consistent with the way God works to impart His hope: "Looking for that blessed hope, and the glorious appearing of the great God and our Savior Jesus Christ" (Titus 2:13).

Of course, not all melodies must be alike all the time. Between excessive rise and excessive fall there are different occasions that call for different moods and styles of music. However, these styles can be achieved without going to extremes and violating the universal nature of God's character.

There is a time for music that is appropriate for mourning, yet that experience should not resemble that of those who have no hope. "But I would not have you to be ignorant, brethren, concerning them which are asleep, that ye sorrow not, even as others which have no hope" (I Thessalonians 4:13).

There is also a time for music that is appropriate for serious self-examination, especially when observing Communion. (See I Corinthians 11:27–32.) David confirmed this when he sang: "Search me, O God, and know my heart: try me, and know my thoughts: And see if there be any wicked way in me . . ." (Psalm 139:23–24). But God does not just leave us to sit in a puddle of self-pity. After examination, repentance, confession, and restitution if necessary, David looks up to his blessed hope in the last phrase of verse 24, ". . . And lead me in the way everlasting."

Static Melody

There is a normal repetition of pitches in melody, but static movement in the melody is a prolonged repetition of pitches, either of a single note or of a motive. If you were to look up from reading this page and sing the phrase *silent night* repeatedly five or six times, you would experience the monotonous feeling of a static repetition in the melody.

A static melody is like having no melody at all. The basic experience of rise and fall, as well as purpose, climax, and fulfillment, is lost. The vitality of the melody is compromised. Unnatural static repetition communicates a chant-like quality that produces first a boring and then a mindless hypnotic effect or trance in the listener. Empty repetition stupefies the mind and closes down the critical functions of the will, which hinders self-control.

Does static melody accurately represent the melody that is in the heart of God? To answer this question, consider the characteristic of static melody and compare that characteristic with the character of God. Static repetition in the melody expresses a mindless lack of control. Is it characteristic of God to be mindless and out of control of His creation? No. One aspect of God's nature is His sovereign control: "The Lord hath prepared his throne in the heavens; and his kingdom ruleth over all" (Psalm 103:19). God is consciously in control of His creation and is working all things together for good to them that love Him. (See Romans 8:28–29.) He is very much in control of His thoughts and is actively prescribing a plan for our lives: "For I know the thoughts that I think toward you, saith the Lord, thoughts of peace, and not of evil, to give you an expected

> The musical message communicated by static melody is the false idea that God is out of touch, indifferent, and not related to the events in our lives.

end" (Jeremiah 29:11). Therefore, static repetition in the melody is not consistent with God's nature. The musical message communicated by static melody is the false idea that God is out of touch, indifferent, and not related to the events in our lives.

Is it God's will for us to be out of control of our senses? No. Neither should the musical messages that we choose to listen to have a hypnotic effect. Because God is sovereign and because we are made in His image, it is God's design for the Holy Spirit to impart self-control to us. One of the evidences of being filled with the Holy Spirit is temperance or self-control. (See Galatians 5:22–23.) Even the prophets did not go into a mindless state when inspired to speak or write under the control of the Holy Spirit: "And the spirits of the prophets are subject to the prophets" (I Corinthians 14:32). There is also a command in Scripture to have self-control over our thoughts: "Casting down imaginations, and every high thing that exalteth itself against the knowledge of God, and bringing into captivity every thought to the obedience of Christ" (II Corinthians 10:5). If we want the fruit of self-control in our hearts, then we should make choices, including music choices, that are consistent with the way God works to impart this control.

The powerful influence of the musical message communicated by static melody is a stupefying surrender to its mind-numbing repetition. The boring effect of the unnecessary repetition of pitches or choruses creates uncertainty and fails to give the listener some expectation of when the song will end. Songs with this characteristic may be referred to as "7 x 11 choruses": 7 words that are repeated 11 times. A good melody will have a definite place near its conclusion that provides a sense of resolution.

> Even the prophets did not go into a mindless state when inspired to speak or write under the control of the Holy Spirit.

While uncertainty is a part of all of our lives, is it God's will for us to live with no sense of closure? No. Neither should the message in the melody line diminish the final sense of closure. What Biblical teaching about God is denied by this perversion of the melody? "Looking unto Jesus the author and finisher of our faith; who for the joy that was set before him endured the cross, despising the shame, and is set down at the right hand of the throne of God" (Hebrews 12:2). Jesus is not only the Author but also the final Finisher of our faith. And the fact that He is set down at the right hand of the throne of God brings to closure all doubt about His ultimate, final authority: "I am Alpha and Omega, the beginning and the ending, saith the Lord, which is, and which was, and which is to come, the Almighty" (Revelation 1:8).

Excessive static repetition communicates the message of those who say, "Where is the promise of his coming? for since the fathers fell asleep, all things continue as they were from the beginning of the creation" (II Peter 3:4). To intentionally create a sense of prolonged uncertainty is to communicate a message that denies the final return of Christ. Instead, our lives are to be lived in anticipation of the end time's promise, when Christ shall rule all nations: "And she brought forth a man child, who was to rule all nations with a rod of iron: and her child was caught up unto God, and to his throne" (Revelation 12:5).

Sliding Notes

A sliding note is either a higher or lower pitch that slides into the melody note. A sliding note may also begin at a melody note and slide away from it to either a higher or lower pitch. Thus, a sliding note is an indirect way to reach or leave the melody note. It is not distinct. It is a distortion of the melody note that loosens the melody line and can contort the message of the music.

God is a God of definite plans and precise purposes. His clearest, most loving pattern was reserved for mankind because He has predestined us to be conformed to the image of His Son: "For whom he did foreknow, he also did predestinate to be conformed to the image of his Son . . ." (Romans 8:29). At this very moment God is actively molding us into this precise pattern: "But we all, with open face beholding as in a glass the glory of the Lord, are changed into the same image from glory to glory, even as by the Spirit of the Lord" (II Corinthians 3:18). It is possible to know what His image is like by the character qualities He commands us to embrace or to avoid. For example, one quality He commands us to avoid is slackness (carelessness): "When thou shalt vow a vow unto the Lord thy God, thou shalt not slack to pay it: for the Lord thy God will surely require it of thee; and it would be sin in thee" (Deuteronomy 23:21). Again, He tells us to not be half-hearted and lukewarm: "I know thy works, that thou art neither cold nor hot: I would thou wert cold or hot. So then because thou art lukewarm, and neither cold nor hot, I will spue thee out of my mouth" (Revelation 3:15–16). God is a great King Who is not pleased with the corruption of carelessness and half-heartedness in worship. (See Malachi 1:14.) He has given us His very best in His Son. He is worthy of our very best. He is worthy of excellence in every area of life and tells us to love Him with a perfect heart that does not selfishly hold anything back from Him. (See I Chronicles 29:9, II Chronicles 16:9, and Matthew 22:37.)

> It is possible to know what His image is like by the character qualities He commands us to embrace or to avoid.

Frequent use of sliding notes creates a sense of looseness, slackness, and carelessness in music. Do sliding notes accurately represent the melody that is in the heart of God? To answer this question, consider the characteristic of sliding notes and compare that characteristic with the character of God. Sliding notes express slackness. Is it characteristic of God to be slack? No. "The Lord is not slack concerning his promise, as some men count slackness . . ." (II Peter 3:9). Therefore, sliding notes in the melody are not consistent with God's nature. The musical message communicated by sliding notes is the false idea that God may be approached in a careless, carefree manner. (See Exodus 3:4–5 and Hebrews 10:30–31.)

Notice that every occurrence of the word *slide* in the Bible is associated with sliding away from God, never toward Him. Consider these examples: "Judge me, O Lord; for I have walked in mine integrity: I have trusted also in the Lord; therefore I shall not slide" (Psalm 26:1). "Therefore we ought to give the more earnest heed to the things which we have heard, lest at any time we should let them slip" (Hebrews 2:1). Remember, truth may be communicated in words or in musical form. Therefore, we ought to give the more earnest heed to the things that we know about God and make sure that our music agrees with what we know of Him in spirit and in truth.

Is it God's will for us to be careless and lax? No. Neither should the message in the melody notes communicate carelessness by repeated occurrences of sliding notes. What Biblical truth is being violated by this perversion of the melody? "See then that ye walk circumspectly, not as fools, but as wise" (Ephesians 5:15). The Greek word for *circumspectly* is *akribos* [#199], which means "exactly." Other meanings of *circumspectly* are "diligently" and "perfectly," as in being precise. Thus, when applied to music, *circumspectly* would mean hitting the note exactly rather than sliding into it. Consider how Paul walked: "I press toward the mark for the prize of the high calling of God in Christ Jesus" (Philippians 3:14). Can you sense Paul's deep love for the Lord and pursuit of excellence? Paul pressed toward the mark! He did not nonchalantly stroll toward the mark.

Excessive use of sliding notes can create such a sense of looseness that it encourages lax moral standards and arouses sensuality. Sliding notes are widely used in businesses of ill repute to arouse sensual sexual desires. The prolonged time it takes to hit the melody note parallels the prolonged undressing, and that is precisely why this type of music is played there. Scripture speaks of singing as an harlot: ". . . After the end of seventy years shall Tyre sing as an harlot. Take an harp, go about the city, thou harlot that hast been forgotten; make sweet melody, sing many songs . . ." (Isaiah 23:15–16). Tyre is likened to a harlot who attracts notice by her song and because of her careless and loose morals admits anyone merely for the sake of gain.

> Sliding notes are widely used in businesses of ill repute to arouse sensual sexual desires.

Sliding notes are used extensively in the world to arouse sensuality. But is it God's will for our sensual desires to be aroused in worship songs? No. God forbid! Neither should the message in the melody notes communicate carelessness by repeated occurrences of sliding notes. "Marriage is honorable in all, and the bed undefiled: but whoremongers and adulterers God will judge" (Hebrews 13:4).

In songs where a single syllable is sung to multiple notes, each note should be hit distinctly without sliding. Hitting individual notes communicates the message that one's yea is yea and his nay is nay: ". . . But let your yea be yea; and your nay, nay; lest ye fall into condemnation" (James 5:12).

The next time you hear a song, notice if the singer or the instruments slide rather than hit the notes precisely. When you sing, are sliding notes part of your singing style? If so, what is your motive? Do you pattern your singing style after the character of God, after the style of others, or after your personal preference?

Do you understand that there is a message in the melody (rising, falling, static, sliding) as well as in the words? Do you agree that the musical messages in the melody should be consistent with the nature of God? Do you agree that the moral messages in the melody must support the Biblical message in the words?

2. HARMONY

When a single note in the melody is played, other notes may be played simultaneously. These notes (including the melody note) that are played at the same time form a chord. Harmony is the sound that is generated when a chord is played. Thus, harmony complements the melody. Harmony adds richness to the melody and makes it more pleasing to the ear. The perception of depth, perspective, and atmosphere is joined to the melody through harmony. If the notes in a chord clash, the harmony is dissonant; if they join and sound good together, the harmony is consonant.

The English word *harmony* is from the Greek word *harmos* [#719 from #716], and it means "joining place." This word is used in the New Testament in Hebrews 4:12: "For the word of

God is quick, and powerful, and sharper than any two edged sword, piercing even to the dividing asunder of soul and spirit, and of the joints and marrow, and is a discerner of the thoughts and intents of the heart." Here the word *harmos* is translated as *joints*. Just as joints are places where bones join together, so harmonies are places where musical tones join together.

Harmony is one of those things that do not need to be studied before it is appreciated. It is usually easy to tell when notes clash or when they blend together in harmony. The basic ability to discern dissonance and consonance is given to us by nature and nature's God. And just as we may grow and mature in our perception and understanding of other attributes of God's nature, so we may mature in our perception and understanding of dissonance and consonance. The basic ability to discern notes that sound good together from notes that clash has been established by God through His design of sound and the human ear. The distinction between dissonance and consonance has not been arbitrarily defined by a committee of musicians on the basis of mere human consensus.

In addition to dissonance and consonance, another aspect of harmony is chord progression. It is not essential to understand the details of chord progression that are explained in the following paragraphs. However, if you spend some time studying this topic or talking with someone who has experience with music, you will discover that chord progression depicts a beautiful analogy.

A musical scale is defined simply as a series of eight sequential notes. Remember that each note by itself is a melody note and that a group of notes played together with one of these melody notes is a chord. So within this scale of eight notes, each individual melody note can be played in a chord.

Now, not only do the sounds within a single chord interact with each other at a given instant, but when played one after the other the sound of the chords within the progression also interact with each other. Here is how that inter-action works. The playing of chords one after the other in sequence is called chord progression, because the order in which the chords are played actually gives the listener a sense of where the music is going—how it is progressing. The sounds these chords make as they are played in sequence will create either a sense of moving toward resolution or away from resolution.

> There is a precisely defined pattern by which the sound of each of these other chords progresses closer and closer to the tonal center.

The chord associated with the very first of the eight notes in a scale is called the tonal center or the place of resolution. For example, in the scale for the key of C, which is made up of these eight notes: C, D, E, F, G, A, B, and C, the chord built on the C note is called the tonal center. The sound of each of the other chords in the C scale (the D, E, F, G, A, and B chords) deviates in varying degrees from the sound of the tonal center.

Now here is the beauty of God's design in tonal progression. There is a precisely defined pattern by which the sound of each of these other chords progresses closer and closer to the tonal center.

To help identify this pattern in the C scale, let's assign a number to each note/chord of the C scale as follows: C=1, D=2,

E=3, F=4, G=5, A=6, and B=7. The sequential progression of this pattern is always **3-6-(2 or 4)-(5 or 7)-1**. E (3) is the chord whose sound is most distant from the tonal center, which is C (1). A (6) is the chord whose sound is next closest to the tonal center after E, followed by either D (2) or F (4), which is equally distant from the tonal center. The two chords whose sound is equally closest to the tonal center of the C scale are G (5) and B (7).

Therefore, if you were to listen to the chord progression of E-D-G-C in the C scale, numbered 3-2-5-1 in the sequential pattern, you would sense the sound of each chord in that progression moving closer and closer toward the tonal center. This chord progression brings resolution.

If you were to listen to the chord progression C-F-E in the C scale, numbered 1-4-3 in the sequential pattern, you would sense the sound of each chord in that progression moving further and further away from the tonal center. That chord progression builds tension. When the last chord played in a musical piece is the tonal center, then final resolution is achieved. The tonal center is home or the place of rest. The amazing fact is that the same orderly progression of 3-6-(2 or 4)-(5 or 7)-1 applies to every key's scale.

For example, in the G scale, illustrated as GABCDEF#G, the tonal center is G. If the equivalent numbering scheme is applied (G=1, A=2, B=3, C=4, D=5, E=6, and F#=7), then the exact same pattern of chord progression occurs in the G scale. In other words, the sequential pattern in which the sound of each of the chords in the G scale progresses closer and closer to the tonal center is also **3-6-(2 or 4)-(5 or 7)-1**, the same pattern as for the C scale. This sequential pattern is identical for every musical scale.

Did someone in a distant culture create this pattern? The answer is emphatically—yes! That Someone is God, and that distant culture is heaven. All physical sound is made up of frequencies in the harmonic series that were created by our musical God.

God designed harmonic frequencies, and He designed the human ear to naturally sense resolution and rest as harmonic sounds move to the tonal center. The audible sense of resolution as chords progress to the tonal center is the objective design of God, not a subjective choice of man.

The tonal center, the home and place of rest, is an "audible" picture of God Himself, offering us His rest: "For he that is entered into his rest, he also hath ceased from his own works, as God did from his. Let us labor therefore to enter into that rest, lest any man fall after the same example of unbelief" (Hebrews 4:10–11). Our rest is from God, so let us labor or progress toward that rest. This truth is communicated to us in the message of music by chord progression.

> The tonal center, the home and place of rest, is an "audible" picture of God Himself, offering us His rest.

In addition to chord progression, when any individual tone (note) is sounded, then within that pitch other pitches (overtones or harmonics) can be heard, each in an exact mathematical relationship to the first. These precise mathematical patterns were created by God and are a reflection of the spiritual order within His divine nature.

God is a God of order. The first mention of order in the Old Testament is within the context of sacrifice or worship: "And they came to the place which God had told him of; and Abraham built an altar there, and laid the wood in order, and bound Isaac his son, and laid him on the altar upon the wood" (Genesis 22:9). This same order was later commanded in the temple worship: "And the sons of Aaron the priest shall put fire upon the altar, and lay the wood in order upon the fire" (Leviticus 1:7). Elijah followed a similar order at an altar of worship. (See I Kings 18:33)

Order can be seen throughout the tabernacle that God instituted for worship: "Two tenons shall there be in one board, set in order one against another: thus shalt thou make for all the boards of the tabernacle" (Exodus 26:17). The lamps of the candlestick were to be set in order continually. (See Exodus 39:37 and Leviticus 24:4.) The shewbread was to be set in order upon the table. (See Exodus 40:4 and II Chronicles 13:11.) The sacrificial parts were to be laid in order upon the altar. (See Leviticus 1:8.) The entire priesthood is referred to as the order of Melchisedec or the order of Aaron. (See Hebrews 7:11 and Luke 1:8.)

> Because God is a God of order, physical harmonies must be balanced in their design of clashing and blending . . .

God orders the events of history: "And who, as I, shall call, and shall declare it, and set it in order for me, since I appointed the ancient people? and the things that are coming, and shall come, let them show unto them" (Isaiah 44:7). Only God can predict and set in order things to come. All others' predictions are chance, but there is no chance or confusion with God;

everything occurs in the order best fitted to His purposes. God's structure and order can be seen throughout the created world. For example, when a spider plucks a goo-covered strand, the vibration makes the goo collect at ordered intervals so that the spider can step between them and not get stuck in its own web. Another example was documented in the eighteenth century. When a German physicist scattered sand on steel discs, he observed that as he played different notes on the violin, the patterns on the discs also changed, forming shapes found in nature: honeycombs, five-pointed stars, and spirals. [1] *Cymatics* is the name given to this study of patterns of shape evoked by sound. [2]

Harmony is another part of music that can be examined in order to understand the musical nature of God and His moral will. Because God is a God of order, physical harmonies must be balanced in their design of clashing and blending in order to accurately reflect the spiritual harmonies in the heart of God. Let's look at how balance or imbalance in dissonance and consonance communicates a message that is consistent or inconsistent with God's nature and His will.

Dissonance

Dissonance is a clashing of notes or chords that introduces a natural tension. Dissonance disturbs the listener and arouses a sense of awareness and alertness. It grabs attention. A normal dissonance in the harmony creates a normal sense of tension, just as some tension is a natural part of caring and concern in life.

Because a spiritual harmony exists in the heart of God, a spiritual dissonance also exists in His heart. One example of spiritual tension in the heart of God is the tension between His love and His holiness. God loves us, cares for us, and does not want to punish us, yet He is holy and must punish sin. Scripture vividly describes how God loved Israel and did not want to punish them, yet He had to punish their sin, so with a normal sense of tension He sought for a man to stand in the gap before Him: "And I sought for a man among them, that should make up the hedge, and stand in the gap before me for the land, that I should not destroy it: but I found none" (Ezekiel 22:30).

With a sense of divine alertness, God is contemplating all the ways of man: "For the ways of man are before the eyes of the LORD, and he pondereth all his goings" (Proverbs 5:21). His watchful, caring eyes are described as running throughout the earth with a normal sense of tension and expectation: "For the eyes of the LORD run to and fro throughout the whole earth, to shew himself strong in the behalf of them whose heart is perfect toward him" (II Chronicles 16:9).

However, excessive dissonance in the harmony builds high tension through disorder and disarray. Excessive clashing of the notes or chords can disrupt the listener and be an influence in stirring up confusion, restlessness, alarm, and rebellion. Details of how worldly music is a contributing factor to delinquent behavior will be given in Chapter 11.

Does excessive dissonance accurately represent the harmony that is in the heart of God? To answer this question, consider the characteristic of excessive dissonance in the harmony, and compare that characteristic with the character of God. Excessive dissonance in the harmony expresses chaos and restlessness. Is turmoil characteristic of God? No. Excessive dissonance communicates a message that is inconsistent with the very nature of the Holy Spirit, Who is described as the Comforter: "But the Comforter, which is the Holy Ghost, whom the Father will send in my name, he shall teach you all things . . ." (John 14:26). The churches mentioned in the New Testament experienced this characteristic of the Holy Spirit: "Then had the churches rest throughout all Judaea and Galilee and Samaria, and were edified; and walking in the fear of the Lord, and in the comfort of the Holy Ghost, were multiplied" (Acts 9:31). God is not restless: "Peace I leave with you, my peace I give unto you: not as the world giveth, give I unto you . . ." (John 14:27). Excessive dissonance in the harmony is not consistent with God's nature.

> Excessive dissonance communicates a message that is inconsistent with the very nature of the Holy Spirit, Who is described as the Comforter.

Is it God's will for us to live with excessive tension and restlessness? No. Neither should the message in the harmony create excessive tension. The imbalance of excessive dissonance in the harmony contradicts the Biblical truth that God offers rest in Christ: "Come unto me, all ye that labour and are heavy laden [e.g., excessive tension], and I will give you rest" (Matthew 11:28).

The comfort that we currently find in Christ and in the Scriptures inspires us with the reality of our future hope and rest: "For whatsoever things were written aforetime were written for our learning, that we through patience and comfort of the scriptures might have hope" (Romans 15:4). If we want God's comfort in our hearts, then we should make choices, including music choices, that are consistent with the way God works to impart His comfort.

Another Biblical truth that is denied by this perversion of the harmony is the triumph and final return of Christ. God designed chord progression to the tonal home center as a picture of our final progression toward our Heavenly Father. Our tonal home is with Jesus Christ in heaven: "Let not your heart be troubled [e.g., agitated or dissonant]: ye believe in God, believe also in me. In my Father's house are many mansions: if it were not so, I would have told you. I go to prepare a place for you. And if I go and prepare a place for you, I will come again, and receive you unto myself; that where I am, there ye may be also" (John 14:2–3).

We are not to let our heart be troubled, agitated, or dissonant, but instead to progress toward Christ, Who is waiting to receive us unto Himself. Music that is characterized by excessive dissonance and clashing of chords communicates a nonverbal message that is in conflict with the truth of the triumph and final return of Christ. Music with a chaotic emotional message supports a chaotic worldview of no end, no resolution, no order, no God, no judgment, and, conveniently, no absolute morals. We must sing music with a message that supports, not undermines, the verbal message.

> Music with a chaotic emotional message supports a chaotic worldview . . .

Note that if a person were to saturate himself with dissonant chaotic music he may actually reach a state where he likes that sound, similar to the way an alcoholic or drug addict reaches a state where he likes his addiction. ". . . God is not the author of confusion, but of peace, as in all churches of the saints" (I Corinthians 14:33). So, if a person adamantly defends chaotic music and is unwilling to objectively "prove what is acceptable unto the Lord," then the music has simply become a reflection of the moral condition of his heart that results from rejecting the orderly nature of God. In this case, a person must deal with the root issues of the lust of the flesh, the lust of the eyes, and the pride of life before addressing the surface issue of music.

A man's morality will dictate his philosophy and his theology. True freedom is not a license to do what we want; it is the power to do what we ought according to God's design and in harmony with His ways.

Consonance

Consonance is a blending of chords that creates a natural relaxation and a sense of unity and accord. A normal consonance in the harmony creates a normal sense of relaxation, just as some relaxation is a natural part of life.

Because a spiritual harmony exists in the heart of God, a spiritual consonance with a divine unity and accord also exists in His heart. The basis of Israel's religion was an acknowledgement of the unity of God: "Hear, O Israel: The LORD our God is one LORD" (Deuteronomy 6:4). Jesus confirmed this unity in God's heart when He said, "I and my Father are one" (John 10:30). All that Jesus said and did was in agreement with His Heavenly Father: "And he that sent me is with me: the Father hath not left me alone; for I do always those things that please him" (John 8:29). No other man could make such a profound claim, live up to it, and have it generally accepted as true for more than two thousand years.

Excessive consonance blends the chords in the harmony to the extent that it provides no interest in the composition. The lack of contrast relaxes the listener to the point of indifference and apathy. Excessive relaxation lulls the listener into an acceptance of everything by everyone and dulls the need to warn and confront that which is wrong.

Does excessive consonance accurately represent the harmony that is in the heart of God? To answer this question, consider the characteristic of excessive consonance in the harmony and compare that characteristic with the character of God. Excessive consonance in the harmony expresses relaxation to the point of indifference and apathy. Is it characteristic of God to blend all ideas together, to tolerate evil for the sake of oneness? No. One aspect of God's nature is His righteousness. There is a righteous standard in His judgments: "For true and righteous are his judgments . . ." (Revelation 19:2). There is a clear distinction in His heart between good and evil: "And the LORD God said, Behold, the man is become as one of us, to know good and evil" (Genesis 3:22), and some day He will make a righteous distinction between good and evil: "And shall come forth; they that have done good, unto the resurrection of life; and they that have done evil, unto the resurrection of damnation" (John 5:29; see also Matthew 25:31–34, 41). Therefore, excessive consonance in the harmony is not consistent with God's nature. Excessive consonance in the harmony communicates a musical message that misrepresents the righteous nature of God.

Is it God's will for us to live with a sense of excessive relaxation? No. Neither should the message in the harmony reflect excessive consonance. The doctrinal truth that is violated by the imbalance of excessive consonance in the harmony is the believer's death to sin: "What shall we say then? Shall we continue in sin, that grace may abound? God forbid. How shall we, that are dead to sin, live any longer therein?" (Romans 6:1–2). We must not continue in sin, must not condone sin, must have no agreement with it, must hate it, and must have no excessive consonance with it.

The emotional, musical message of excessive consonance is a message that rejects the doctrine of sin and man's sin nature. It communicates the

> Excessive consonance in the harmony communicates a musical message that misrepresents the righteous nature of God.

philosophy of "live and let live." No rocking of the boat, no dissonance, is allowed in the pursuit of personal happiness. Excessive consonance communicates a message of peace at any price. No moral absolutes are allowed to get in the way of the compromises that are necessary to achieve this superficial state. It is a superficial state because it ignores the reality of man's sin nature and is based on the pursuit of mere happiness without holiness. Excessive consonance in music supports this indifference toward righteousness and apathy toward evil.

The musical message in excessive consonance communicates a message that nothing is ever wrong, not even obviously sinful practices such as sodomy and abortion. It promotes the false ideas of a universal oneness with an imaginary type of god who simply overlooks wrongs and who has no intention of ever separating the sheep from the goats.

Paul resisted the idea of living in consonance with sin and challenges us to have a driving purpose and passion in striving against it: "Ye have not yet resisted unto blood, striving against sin" (Hebrews 12:4). Jesus likewise calls us to serve Him with righteous passion as well as compassion: "If any man will come after me, let him deny himself, and take up his cross daily, and follow me" (Luke 9:23).

Recall that harmony is the sound that is generated when a chord is played. One online etymology dictionary identifies the musical word *chord* as a shortened version of the word *accord*.[3] The idea of being in one accord with others communicates the same meaning as being in harmony with them: "And they, continuing daily with one accord in the temple, and breaking bread from house to house, did eat their meat with gladness and singleness of heart" (Acts 2:46). This is a one-accord experience of many different individuals coming together in true unity just as a chord is an experience of many different notes sounding good together in consonant harmony.

> In a true one-accord fellowship, every individual member is free to openly and honestly contribute to the whole.

But excessive consonance communicates a false message about unity, where the individual members are not free to give to the Body what God intends that member to give, maybe out of fear of disrupting the unity of the group. If this type of unity is the norm, then it is only a surface fellowship that is for show—it is not real; it is hypocrisy. Excessive consonance in the harmony reflects this emotional sentimentality in the congregation and prideful showmanship in the pulpit.

A false unity does not allow for change and therefore does not allow for growth: "But we all, with open face beholding as in a glass the glory of the Lord, are changed into the same image from glory to glory, even as by the Spirit of the Lord" (II Corinthians 3:18). In a true one-accord fellowship, every individual member is free to openly and honestly contribute to the whole. Each member has freedom to speak, freedom to listen, freedom to wait, and joy in knowing that it is God Who is leading and working all things together for good. "Preach the word; be instant in season, out of season; reprove, rebuke, exhort with all longsuffering and doctrine" (II Timothy 4:2). David also recognized the value of honest confrontation: "Let the righteous smite me; it shall be a kindness: and let him reprove me; it shall be an excellent oil" (Psalm 141:5).

Do you understand that there is a message in the harmony as well as in the words? Do you agree that the musical messages in the harmony should be consistent with the nature of God? Do you agree that the moral messages in the harmony must support the Biblical message in the words?

3. RHYTHM

Because rhythm is associated with the timing of music, we will first define the basic unit for measuring time in music, which is called the beat. A musical beat provides the orderly movement of music through time. By definition, the beat simply refers to equal units of time. A tone may or may not be sounded on each beat.

An example of beat where a tone is sounded on each beat is the ticking of a clock. Each tick (tone) identifies a regular unit of duration (beat). An example of a silent beat where a tone is not sounded on each beat occurs in the phrase "Je-sus loves me; this I know." A single tone is sounded on the word *know*, but that single tone it is held out for the duration of two beats. The beat simply represents equal units of duration in time, not the tone that is sounded on the beat. One can identify the beat by tapping his feet or clapping his hands to help mark the units of time, whether or not a musical tone is sounded. Biblical references to the word *beat* relate to striking something or someone. (See Joel 3:10 and Deuteronomy 25:3.) The word *beat*, in regard to music, has the same general application.

An example of order in music is the organization of time into units known as measures. Each measure contains a fixed number of beats. This fixed number of beats per measure repeats itself in every measure to let everyone know what to expect, to keep everyone together, to eliminate confusion, and to provide order to the music. The beat provides the orderly movement of music through time.

The time signature is what defines this order for a particular piece of music. It appears as a fraction at the beginning of a sheet of music. The top number defines the number of beats there will be in each measure. The bottom number tells the kind of note that will represent one beat. The most common kinds of notes are whole, half, quarter, eighth, and sixteenth notes. Let's now examine the time relationship between these notes.

One way to visualize the duration of each different kind of note is to compare them to corresponding units on a ruler. Just as there are half-, quarter-, and eighth-inch marks in one inch, so there may be half, quarter, and eighth notes in a measure. Let the one-inch mark on a ruler, which is a fixed measure of distance in space, represent the musical measure, which is a fixed measure of duration in time. Though this ruler analogy is not precisely accurate for every time signature, it is provided here as a means to understand the basic concept of time signatures.

> The beat provides the orderly movement of music through time.

In the 4/4 time signature, the top number specifies 4 beats per measure. Just as there are 4 quarter-inch marks to measure distance in one inch, so there are 4 beats to measure time in this musical measure.

In the 4/4 time signature, the bottom number specifies the quarter note (1/4) as the note that gets one beat. In summary, the top number specified a total of 4 beats per measure and the bottom number specified the quarter note as the kind of note that would be sounded for the duration of a single beat. Thus, for a song written in the 4/4 time signature, a series of 4 quarter notes would define the boundary of a musical measure for that song. However, just as two eighth-inch marks may be substituted for a single quarter-inch mark, so two eighth notes may be substituted for a single quarter note. If two eighth notes were substituted for a single quarter note in the above example, then a series of two eighth notes and three quarter notes would define the boundary of that musical measure. This substitution is possible because just as the two eighth-inch marks measure the same distance as the quarter-inch mark, so the two eighth notes sound for the same duration as the quarter note. The only difference is that two short tones are sounded for the same duration as the one longer tone. This notation provides the structure, the expectation, and order that are needed for the congregation, choir, and instruments to all stay together.

With this understanding of the different lengths of duration for the various types of notes, let's define *rhythm* and consider how it is different from the *beat*. The beat refers to the unit of time and not the sounding of tones. The beat simply represents equal units of duration in a fixed period of time. The beat is regular. And, like the repetitious ticking of a clock, if it is the only element of the music that is focused on (identified by clapping or tapping), then it would be very monotonous to listen to.

The rhythm, however, is not always regular but is related to the tones that are heard by the listener when a note is sounded. One kind of note can be held out for a duration longer than one beat, or two notes can be sounded within the duration of a single beat. Thus, rhythm is a pattern of long and short tones. The many combinations of the different kinds of notes that are sounded for different lengths of time create a vast variety of rhythms. Rhythm gives unique expression to beat, even though the endless varieties in the rhythm are all built upon the foundation of a regular beat.

> Rhythm gives unique expression to beat . . .

Note that technically there is a difference between a musical beat and a musical rhythm. However, because *beat* and *rhythm* are so closely related, the two terms are commonly used interchangeably.

In classical Greek, the word *rhythmos* means "measured flow or movement." It is from the Greek word *rhein*, which means "to flow." The word translated *flow* in the New Testament is *rheo* in John 7:38: "He that believeth on me, as the scripture hath said, out of his belly shall flow rivers of living water." In every other place that *rheo* occurs in the Bible, it is translated as *spoken* or *said*, which refers to words flowing from the mouth.

The following discussion of rhythm is helpful but not essential to understanding the message of this book. If you are not familiar with music and would like to learn more about rhythm, two things would assist you with the following explanation: (1) a hymn book to view how the music is laid out on the page of the sample hymn being discussed, and (2) a person (or use a Google search online) to explain the definition of the musical terms *measure*, *time signature*, *half note*, *quarter note*, and *eighth note*. Alternatively, you may consider the analogy of a ruler to follow the main thought. Remember that the one-inch mark on a ruler, which measures the distance moved along in space, represents the musical measure, which measures duration in time.

Look at the song "When We All Get to Heaven." It has a 4/4 time signature, which means there are 4 beats per measure and that the quarter note receives 1 beat (one quarter note represents ¼ inch). We will analyze the second measure, which contains the words *love of Jesus*. The second measure begins with two eighth notes. This is an example of how two tones can be sounded within the duration of a single beat (at this point in the measure there is a total of 1 beat, which can be viewed as two 1/8-inch marks for a total of ¼ inch).

Next in the measure are two more eighth notes. Two separate tones are sounded again within the duration of 1 beat (now there is a total of 2 beats in the measure, which can be viewed as adding two more 1/8-inch marks for a total of ½ inch). Next appears a quarter note, which is the note that is assigned 1 beat per the 4/4 time signature (this brings the total duration of the measure to 3 beats, which can be viewed as adding ¼ inch for a total of ¾ inch). Finally, the last quarter note appears in the measure (the completed duration of the measure is now 4 beats as indicated by the top number 4 in the 4/4 time signature, which can be viewed as adding the last ¼ inch for a total of 1 inch).

Jumping to the fourth measure of this song, we see that it begins with a quarter note (1 beat or ¼ inch). Following this note is another quarter note (bringing the total to 2 beats or ½ inch). Last in this measure is a half note. Because the time signature assigned a single beat to the quarter note, the half note will receive 2 beats. This is an example of how one tone can be held out for a duration longer than 1 beat (adding these 2 beats to the previous 2 brings the total beats for this measure to 4 beats or 1 inch).

There are thousands of songs written with a 4/4 time signature. All songs written with a 4/4 time signature repeat the same time unit of 4 beats per measure. However, these songs vary with a different rhythm, because the note that represents the beat (the quarter note in the bottom of the 4/4 time signature) may be implemented in so many different ways.

For example, the quarter note may appear as itself, it may be represented by two eighth notes, or two quarter notes may be represented by a single half note. And all of these and other variations may appear at different places within a measure. Thus, variation in the duration of the tones that are sounded in a measure, represented by the different kinds of notes, creates a unique expression, which is the rhythm for that measure. Yet, all these 4/4 measures contain the same fixed number of beats per measure.

> The musical message in the rhythm is that there is an orderly, righteous pattern to life as we move through time.

Why is the particular note that represents the beat implemented in the different ways that it is throughout a particular song? One reason is that if a song is written to be sung, the rhythmic pattern is chosen in such a way as to match the inflection (syllables) of the lyrics.

As an exercise for the reader, notice how the different kinds of notes correspond with the words to create the rhythms for the songs "Away in a Manger" and "Onward Christian Soldiers." An orderly rhythm has the power to unite the musical melody with the lyrics. It will unfold the melody and the words together and help those who are singing along to easily sing that song.

The musical message in the rhythm is that there is an orderly, righteous pattern to life as we move through time. This glorious pattern, which God has predestined for each of us, is ". . . to be conformed to the image of his Son . . ." (Romans 8:29). The Apostle Paul gave Titus practical instruction to encourage him to follow this pattern: "In all things shewing thyself a pattern of good works: in doctrine shewing uncorruptness, gravity, sincerity, sound speech, that cannot be condemned; that he that is of the contrary part may be ashamed, having no evil thing to say of you" (Titus 2:7–8). Because a balanced rhythm is decent and orderly, it reflects the nature of God and resonates with the

> **Because God is a God of order, physical rhythms must be balanced in their design of contrast and sameness . . .**

desire for decorum and order in the heart of those created in His image. This type of balanced rhythm will be referred to in this book as the *natural rhythm*. Caution must be taken not to introduce conflicting rhythms that interfere with the natural rhythm or confuse the musical messages in the melody and the verbal messages in the lyrics.

Rhythm is another part of music that can be examined to understand the musical nature of God and His moral will. Because God is a God of order, physical rhythms must be balanced in their design of contrast and sameness in order to accurately reflect the spiritual rhythm in the heart of God. Let's examine how balance or imbalance in variation and repetition communicates a message that is consistent or inconsistent with God's nature and His will.

Variation

A balanced natural rhythm provides orderly movement of the music through time. Variation in the rhythm creates contrast and arouses interest. Natural rhythm allows for variation without distorting the musical message that life has purpose and order and that there is a living God to be followed as one moves through life.

As discussed above, one way to create various kinds of natural rhythms is to vary the time signature, which creates a different number of beats per measure and assigns different types of notes (eighth note, quarter note, etc.) to the note that represents one beat in the measure. For a given time signature, almost a limitless number of possible natural rhythms are available—because of the many ways that different kinds of notes can be assigned to the beats in each measure. Some other ways to introduce variation in the rhythm are to change the tempo or to change the time signature itself during the course of a song.

> Because a spiritual rhythm exists in the heart of God, a spiritual variation with a divine contrast also exists in His heart.

An example of variation in nature is snowflakes. Although they are all six-sided in shape (analogous to a fixed number of beats per measure), there are no two snowflakes exactly the same (analogous to the variety of possible rhythmic patterns).

Likewise, there are no two people exactly the same. "But now hath God set the members every one of them in the body, as it hath pleased him. And if they were all one member, where were the body? But now are they many members, yet but one body" (I Corinthians 12:18–20). One message communicated by the natural variation in the rhythm is the unique and special purpose of every believer within the Body of Christ.

Variation in the rhythm creates a normal tension through a sense of contrast. A normal variation in the rhythm creates a normal sense of contrast, just as some variation is a natural part of life.

Because a spiritual rhythm exists in the heart of God, a spiritual variation with a divine contrast also exists in His heart. There is a divine sense of tension and contrast between many of God's attributes. The opposing qualities of justice and mercy equally reflect His divine nature. (See Psalm 89:14.) Similarly, ". . . his mercy is everlasting; and his truth endureth to all generations" (Psalm 100:5). Within the nature of God is "a man of sorrows" (Isaiah 53:3) and "fullness of joy" (Psalm 16:11). The nature of God includes both a supreme divinity and a glorified humanity: "In the beginning was the Word, and the Word was with God, and the Word was God. . . . And the Word was made flesh, and dwelt among us, (and we beheld his glory, the glory as of the only begotten of the Father,) full of grace and truth" (John 1:1, 14).

However, excessive variation in the rhythm builds high tension through disorder and distraction from the natural rhythm. Excessive variation of the rhythm can disrupt the listener, bringing confusion and bewilderment as competing rhythms stray from the natural rhythmic pattern and compete against it.

Does excessive variation accurately represent the rhythm that is in the heart of God? To answer this question, consider the characteristic of excessive variation in the rhythm and compare that characteristic with the character of God. Excessive variation in the rhythm expresses distraction and confusion.

Is it characteristic of God to be distracted and bewildered? No. Jesus knew Who He was and where He was going. He described Himself as "... the way, the truth, and the life..." (John 14:6). There is no counseling situation that could bewilder the mind of God. God's "... name shall be called Wonderful, Counselor ..." (Isaiah 9:6). He is "... the only wise God ..." (I Timothy 1:17). Even Jesus' critics marveled at His wisdom. (See John 7:46.) God's thoughts and purposes are clear and precise. God is not scatter-brained and easily distracted from His purposes: "For my thoughts are not your thoughts, neither are your ways my ways, saith the LORD. For as the heavens are higher than the earth, so are my ways higher than your ways, and my thoughts than your thoughts" (Isaiah 55:8–9). Paul marveled at the wisdom and ways of God: "O the depth of the riches both of the wisdom and knowledge of God! how unsearchable are his judgments, and his ways past finding out!" (Romans 11:33). Therefore, excessive variation in the rhythm is not consistent with God's nature.

> God is not scatter-brained and easily distracted from His purposes . . .

Is it God's will for us to be vexed with excessive distractions? No. Neither should the musical messages in the rhythm reflect excessive variation. Excessive variation in the rhythm not only misrepresents God's divine nature but soon distracts the listener from decorum, modesty, and propriety. Excessive variation in the rhythm leads the listener away from the Scriptural admonition to "let all things be done decently and in order" (I Corinthians 14:40).

Scripture describes our human tendency to go astray: "All we like sheep have gone astray; we have turned every one to his own way . . ." (Isaiah 53:6). Excessive variation and irregularity in the rhythm disrupt the movement of the music through time. It communicates the lie of humanism that life has no purpose and that there is no God to be followed. The confusion leads to selfish wanderings and a lifestyle of doing as you please. These attitudes are expressed in the words of a 1972 hit song, *Garden Party*, by Rick Nelson: "You can't please everyone, so you've got to please yourself." [4]

As we will see in Chapter 9, secular humanism teaches that the only way to find meaning in life is not through following God's Word but rather through the confusing evolutionary process of compromising and synthesizing together conflicting ideas. Scripture clearly admonishes us to beware of the distracting and chaotic messages communicated by every wind of doctrine: "That we henceforth be no more children, tossed to and fro, and carried about with every wind of doctrine, by the sleight of men, and cunning craftiness, whereby they lie in wait to deceive" (Ephesians 4:14). It is just as important to not be deceived and led astray by the chaotic emotional messages communicated by the distraction of excessive variation in the rhythm.

The emotional message of aimless wanderings communicated by distracting rhythms is described in Scripture as an idle

> Satan will try to preoccupy us with trivial eddy currents that swirl in meaningless circles alongside God's will for us.

lifestyle: "And withal they learn to be idle, wandering about from house to house; and not only idle, but tattlers also and busybodies, speaking things which they ought not" (I Timothy 5:13). The Greek word for *idle* is *argos* [#692], which means "lazy or useless." They wander about because they are distracted from any meaningful life purpose.

If those who "learn to be idle" are not led to repentance and fulfillment in Christ, then they will wax worse and worse into greater degrees of defiant living: "But evil men and seducers shall wax worse and worse, deceiving, and being deceived" (II Timothy 3:13). If distracting rhythms are not corrected, they will also wax worse and worse into greater degrees of disorder and chaos.

> We should not be asking what is wrong with these techniques . . . but rather what is right with them.

The winds of doctrine will become raging waves: "Raging waves of the sea, foaming out their own shame; wandering stars, to whom is reserved the blackness of darkness for ever" (Jude 1:13). It is not uncommon at all to hear testimonies of how listening to softer styles of worldly music gradually led to a wandering desire for harder and harder forms of worldly music.

If Satan cannot defeat us, he will distract us from the main stream of God's will for our lives. Satan will try to preoccupy us with trivial eddy currents that swirl in meaningless circles alongside God's will for us.

There are four techniques being used in the music of the world today to create excessive variation and distraction from the natural rhythm. If we love God with all our heart and desire

His best for our life, our family, and our church, we should not be asking what is wrong with these techniques before we reject them, but rather we should be asking what is right with them before we accept them. This practice would provide a guard against the danger of quenching the Holy Spirit. (See I Thessalonians 5:19.)

Worldly Rhythms

A dominant rhythm is one of the basic characteristics of various kinds of worldly music. The dominant rhythm is usually accompanied by a high tension created by accented syncopation, back-beats, break-beats, and poly-rhythms.

Syncopation

To accent a beat is to place an emphasis on that beat. Examples of accented beats in natural rhythm are the first and third beats in a 4/4 time signature as described earlier.

> It does not take very much syncopation to introduce the tension, distraction, and confusion that are so characteristic of the moral confusion that permeates our culture.

However, when accents are shifted away from the expected beat, they create distraction in a composition. This shifting is called syncopation. Syncopation occurs whenever an accent that the listener expects is left out and instead is inserted in a place where it is normally not expected.

Care must be taken if syncopation is used, because it does not take very much syncopation to introduce the tension, distraction, and confusion that are so characteristic of the moral confusion that permeates our culture. Therefore, the balance of regular accent patterns and occasional syncopation does not necessarily mean equal amounts. For example, in a balanced diet, equal amounts of spices and vegetables could not be eaten. Syncopation must be used sparingly if it is used at all.

Back-beat

Back-beat is a form of syncopation that constantly shifts the accent away from the normally accented beats to beats that are not normally accented. It is far more intense than occasional syncopation, because it creates a sensation of constant syncopation. In 4/4 time, this worldly rhythm would emphasize the second and fourth beats in direct contradiction to the normal accent on the first and third beats.

This constant back-beat creates a separate rhythm that is contrary to the natural rhythmic order. Recall how the natural rhythm supports the melody and harmony and helps them flow together with any lyrics in the natural way it is designed to do. Because the rhythm created by the back-beat is contrary to the natural rhythm and is in direct opposition to it, it introduces a great amount of disorder and distraction and communicates an emotional message of resistance and rebellion that is contrary to the messages in the melody and lyrics.

Notice how those involved in the music of the world recognize the connection between the back-beat and evil spirits. Mickey Hart, drummer for the Grateful Dead, said that rock and roll is "the latest extension of the African backbeat." He also said, "It is hard to pinpoint the exact moment when I awoke to the fact that my tradition—rock and roll—did have a spirit side, that there was a branch of the family that had maintained the ancient connection between the drum and the gods."[5] In a 1982 interview with Jerry Lee Lewis, an American rock and roll singer, researcher Steve Turner asked what power falls on Jerry Lee when he performs. Lewis replied, "The power of voodoo."[6]

The fact that Satan can distort order is confirmed by the way he distorts other aspects of God's designs, such as miracles. The book of Revelation describes an evil beast that "doeth great wonders, so that he maketh fire come down from heaven on the earth in the sight of men, and deceiveth them that dwell on the earth by the means of those miracles which he had power to do . . ." (Revelation 13:13–14; see also Revelation 16:14). Because Satan is a master deceiver, we must remain alert to all his deceptions, including those in musical rhythms.

> Notice how those involved in music of the world recognize the connection between the back-beat and evil spirits.

There are some who do not acknowledge the existence and work of evil spirits. Those who are more worldly-minded than they are spiritually minded run a greater risk of being deceived by styles and innovations in music, because they are not alert to Satan's deceptions. The more that the light of the glorious gospel of Christ is suppressed in our culture, then the easier it will be for evil spirits to manipulate and deceive. The Apostle John exhorts us to test the spirits: "Beloved, believe not every spirit, but try the spirits whether they are of God . . ." (I John 4:1).

The righteous use of rhythm is not determined by what is personally pleasing but rather by what Scripture reveals about the nature of God. Only within those righteous bounds is there room for unique personal preferences.

Break-beat

Break-beat is another form of syncopation that breaks the pattern of the natural rhythm. It is repetitive like the back-beat, but it is different than the back-beat in that the accents occur between the normal beats. In 4/4 time, this worldly rhythm would introduce additional accents between the four beats, for example, placing accents on the second half of each beat. Thus, break-beat is another direct challenge to the regular accent of the natural rhythm and further intensifies disorder, disturbance, and distraction from the natural rhythm, communicating musical messages of carelessness, wildness, and casting off of restraint.

The term *break-dancing* is thought to have originated from its relation to the *break-beat*, and the term *breaking* was street slang for "acting energetically" or "causing a disturbance."[7] The performance of a break-dancer may demonstrate great arm strength for support and balance as he performs skillful moves. However, such physical skill does not justify the associated messages in the break-beat of the music, just as a bank robber's skill would not justify the associated lies of his covetous belief system.

The righteousness of a skill is not determined by how well it is performed in comparison to others but rather by how well it aligns with God's will and purposes. Likewise, the true value of performing to a break-beat through a dance or on an instrument is not determined by the skill of the performer but rather by what Scripture reveals about the nature of that type of rhythm.

Poly-rhythm

A poly-rhythm is the simultaneous sounding of two or more independent rhythms. Poly-rhythms require at least two rhythms to be played concurrently. The rhythms with a greater number of beats per measure are played faster than the rhythms with a fewer number of beats per measure so that they all finish at the same time. The result of overlaying multiple rhythmic patterns is the creation of multiple occurrences of break-beats. This is such a flagrant disruption of the natural rhythm that it could be described only as distracting, confusing, and openly rebellious.

It is no coincidence that the defiance and rebellion characteristic of the 1960s was associated with and supported by these types of rhythmic disorders in worldly music. In the late 1960s the Beatles stated, "Our music is capable of causing emotional instability, disorganized behavior, rebellion, and even revolution."[8] Columnist Phyllis Schlafly tells of a letter she received from professional musician Jack Staulcup. She reported in 1978: "According to Staulcup, a steady diet of rock and roll junk promotes degenerate rebelliousness among teenagers. . . . Staulcup concludes that rock and roll is the biggest legalized racket this country has ever seen. If we value civilization, we cannot afford to ignore any longer the high correlation between the multibillion dollar hard rock racket and the explosion of drug use and illicit sex among their teenage victims."[9]

When Saul attempted to worship God in the way of his own choosing, Samuel gave him a sharp rebuke: "For rebellion is as the sin of witchcraft, and stubbornness is as iniquity and idolatry. Because thou hast rejected the word of the LORD, he hath also rejected thee from being king" (I Samuel 15:23). Rebellion is like the sin of witchcraft, because in both there is a movement out from under God's order, design, and protection and direct exposure to Satan's influence and control. Could it be that because the modern Church has rejected God's order in music that God is withholding the revival that is so desperately needed? We will address this topic further in Chapters 8 and 11.

The confusion of these worldly rhythmic variations does nothing to enhance the natural rhythmic order and melody of the music. Instead, they combine to create such dominance in the rhythm that the melody, harmony, and lyrics are overridden and often unrecognizable.

This is exactly what sin seeks to do. Sin seeks to have dominion over us: "Let not sin therefore reign in your mortal body, that ye should obey it in the lusts thereof. Neither yield ye your members as instruments of unrighteousness unto sin: but yield yourselves unto God, as those that are alive from the dead, and your members as instruments of righteousness unto God. For sin shall not have dominion over you: for ye are not under the law, but under grace" (Romans 6:12–14). For sin to have dominion over us it must find a way into our lives. One way into

> It is no coincidence that the defiance and rebellion characteristic of the 1960s was associated with and supported by the rhythmic disorders in worldly music.

our lives is through our ears. To avoid yielding our members as instruments of unrighteousness would include not yielding our ears to listen to those sounds that are designed to contradict God's holy and orderly nature.

Music of the world aids the expression of the flesh, which is at war with the Spirit: "For the flesh lusteth against the Spirit, and the Spirit against the flesh: and these are contrary the one to the other: so that ye cannot do the things that ye would" (Galatians 5:17). The emotional messages in worldly rhythms breed a worldly lifestyle that hinders Christlike living and distracts from the meaningful experience of living in the center of God's will. The choices we make, including music choices, have consequences: "And if ye walk contrary unto me, and will not hearken unto me; I will bring seven times more plagues upon you according to your sins" (Leviticus 26:21).

> We cannot afford to ignore the high correlation between the multibillion dollar hard rock racket and the explosion of drug use and illicit sex among their teenage victims.

We will see in Chapter 10 how these rhythmic techniques produce an adrenaline rush that becomes addictive. And like other addictions, it creates a liking for the very thing that tyrannizes and brings into bondage. The Bible warns about the deceitfulness of sin, which offers temporary pleasures with hidden consequences: "Choosing rather to suffer affliction with the people of God, than to enjoy the pleasures of sin for a season" (Hebrews 11:25). "There is a way which seemeth right unto a man, but the end thereof are the ways of death" (Proverbs 14:12).

Repetition

A balanced natural rhythm provides orderly movement of the music through time. While variation in the rhythm creates contrast and interest, repetition creates constancy and predictability.

Natural rhythm provides repetition by making the first beat of a measure a strong beat, called a *down beat* or *accent*. In a 4/4 time signature, the strong accent on the first beat is called the primary accent. A milder accent that is placed on the third beat is called the secondary accent. This accent on every first and third beat of a measure provides a natural order and regularity to the rhythm. It keeps everyone moving along—moving along together instead of dragging behind or rushing ahead.

Notice the accent on the first beat of each measure in the song "Fairest Lord Jesus." This repetition in the rhythm creates a sensation of order, familiarity, expectation, and relaxation. If we have done something repeatedly in the past, then we are familiar with it and are more able to relax as we do it.

Repetition creates a natural relaxation through a sense of familiarity and expectation. A normal repetition in the rhythm creates a normal sense of relaxation, just as some relaxation is a natural part of life.

Because a spiritual rhythm exists in the heart of God, a spiritual repetition with a divine expectation and consistency also exists in His heart. The very definition of character includes the concept of consistency. If a person is said to have a particular character quality, it is because, independent of circumstances, he is so consistent in demonstrating this quality that he is said to be characterized by it. God can be counted on to consistently demonstrate the character quality of love, because "God is love . . ." (I John 4:16b). We do not deserve God's mercies, yet they are faithfully new every morning. (See Lamentations 3:22–23.) God can be expected to always act in a way that is consistent with His divine nature: "For I am the Lord, I change not . . ." (Malachi 3:6). "Jesus Christ the same yesterday, and to day, and for ever" (Hebrews 13:8).

Excessive repetition in the rhythm tends to induce excessive relaxation. An extreme example of excessive rhythmic repetition would be a song in which every measure consists of two half notes. When the same rhythmic pattern is repeated excessively without variation, the monotonous repetition of the hypnotic pattern dulls the senses to the point of thoughtless lowering of restraint and careless disregard for self-control. Those who give instructions on how to perform the mindless worldly practice of hypnosis state that repetition is a key factor. [10]

Does excessive repetition in the rhythm accurately represent the rhythm that is in the heart of God? To answer this question, consider the characteristic of excessive repetition in the rhythm and compare that characteristic with the character of God. Excessive repetition in the rhythm expresses thoughtlessness and carelessness. Is it characteristic of God to be thoughtless and uncaring? No. In His warning about vain repetitions, Jesus described God as a thoughtful Father Who cares about our needs: "Be not ye therefore like unto them: for your Father knoweth what things ye have need of, before ye ask him" (Matthew 6:8). God not only knows about our needs, but He also sincerely cares about them: "If ye then, being evil, know how to give good gifts unto your children, how much more shall your

Father which is in heaven give good things to them that ask him?" (Matthew 7:11). "Casting all your care upon him; for he careth for you" (I Peter 5:7). Therefore, excessive repetition in the rhythm is not consistent with God's nature. Instead of communicating a musical message of a personal God Who cares, excessive repetition in the rhythm communicates a musical message of a god who is distant and indifferent—who requires much repetition to be heard.

Has God established a balanced measure of consistency and repetition for our lives? Yes. This is demonstrated for us in the Bible by the concept of godly customs: "And when he was twelve years old, they went up to Jerusalem after the custom of the feast" (Luke 2:42). God has also commanded us to "remember the sabbath day, to keep it holy" (Exodus 20:8). Paul established godly traditions in the early churches: "Now we command you, brethren, in the name of our Lord Jesus Christ, that ye withdraw yourselves from every brother that walketh disorderly, and not after the tradition which he received of us" (II Thessalonians 3:6). The musical messages communicated in the natural rhythm affirm this aspect of God's design.

> Because a spiritual rhythm exists in the heart of God, a spiritual repetition with a divine expectation and consistency also exists in His heart.

However, is it God's will for us to practice vain repetitions and mindless tradition? No. Neither should the message in the rhythm reflect mind-numbing repetition. Jesus instructs us to avoid the fallacy of heathen repetitions: "But when ye pray, use not vain repetitions, as the heathen do: for they think that they shall be heard for their much speaking. Be not ye therefore like unto them . . ." (Matthew 6:7–8).

One form of excessive repetition is to accent every beat with the same strong emphasis as the first beat, creating what is referred to as a dominant beat. This booming repetition interferes with the natural rhythmic patterns and dominates rather than supports the melody and words. It also induces a hypnotic effect. The mindless effect of excessive repetition not only misrepresents God's nature, but it also lowers restraint and self-control, thus arousing and intensifying sensuality, which is contrary to God's nature.

For example, an article that describes lewd dancing says: "Remember that your moves need to flow with the song to make the act more sensual. Songs with a repeated beat are easy to dance to." It then states: "Feel one with the beats and think that the music has taken control over your body."[11] Note the instruction to intentionally set aside self-control, aided by the repeated beat. The hypnotic effect of excessive repetition stirs up lust that will take control over one's body.

> A dominant rhythm, along with other techniques such as sliding notes and static melody, can arouse sensuality in the emotions independent of the lyrics.

A dominant rhythm, along with other techniques such as sliding notes and static melody, can arouse sensuality in the emotions independent of the lyrics. The Apostle Paul warns believers not to walk as those who have given themselves over to lasciviousness: "Who being past feeling have given themselves over unto lasciviousness, to work all uncleanness with greediness" (Ephesians 4:19). The Greek word for *lasciviousness* is *aselgeia* [#766], which means "wantonness." Those who are lascivious are so past natural caution that they have dulled their senses and are without restraint in arousing within themselves desires that cannot be righteously fulfilled.

Paul also gives a strong warning about defrauding fellow believers: "That no man go beyond and defraud his brother in any matter: because that the Lord is the avenger of all such, as we also have forewarned you and testified" (I Thessalonians 4:6). The word *defraud* is from the Greek word *pleonekteo* [#4122], which means "to overreach, or take advantage of others." Those who defraud arouse within others desires that cannot be righteously fulfilled.

A bad habit is an example of repetitive behavior that can be reinforced by the dominant repetition of the rhythm.

A bad habit is an example of repetitive behavior that can be reinforced by the dominant repetition of the rhythm. A dominant rhythm excites the sin nature and lowers the restraint and self-control that are needed to conquer habits. "Let not sin therefore reign in your mortal body, that ye should obey it in the lusts thereof. Neither yield ye your members as instruments of unrighteousness unto sin: but yield yourselves unto God, as those that are alive from the dead, and your members as instruments of righteousness unto God. For sin shall not have dominion [be dominant] over you: for ye are not under the law, but under grace" (Romans 6:12–14).

Do you understand that there is a message in the rhythm as well as in the words? Do you agree that the musical messages in the rhythm should be consistent with the nature of God? Do you agree that the moral messages in the rhythm must support the Biblical message in the words?

In your next music selection, are you willing to test the moral message of the rhythm to prove whether or not it is consistent with Biblical principles?

CHAPTER 6

Applying Biblical Principles of Separation

THIS CHAPTER EXAMINES THE PRINCIPLE of not being unequally yoked together: "Be ye not unequally yoked together with unbelievers: for what fellowship hath righteousness with unrighteousness? and what communion hath light with darkness?" (II Corinthians 6:14). A godly lifestyle should not be unequally yoked with a worldly musical style.

1. DO NOT IMITATE WORLDLY METHODS

It has been observed that imitation is a form of admiration. Because righteousness has no fellowship with unrighteousness and no admiration of unrighteousness, there is no place in the Christian life for imitating worldly ways. This section contains several lengthy passages of Scripture. Please take the time to carefully read each of these passages from God's holy Word.

Let's look at a Biblical example of the danger of copying worldly ways. The approach used in viewing this example is the same approach Paul used in showing how specific Old Testament laws are based on universal life principles. From I

Timothy 5:17–18 and Deuteronomy 25:4, we learn that Paul found in the instructions about rewarding an ox for its labor a higher law and basic principle of rewarding spiritual leaders for their labor. This Old Testament law was not given just for the ox but was primarily given to those who are spiritually minded so that they might understand the higher moral law behind it and its application throughout history. (See I Corinthians 9:6–11.)

In the same way, let's consider another Biblical principle of life that has application to music today. It is an example of the danger of copying worldly ways that occurred when the Philistines returned the ark to Israel: "And the ark of the Lord was in the country of the Philistines seven months. And the Philistines called for the priests and the diviners, saying, What shall we do to the ark of the Lord? tell us wherewith we shall send it to his place. And they said, If ye send away the ark of the God of Israel, send it not empty; but in any wise return him a trespass offering: then ye shall be healed, and it shall be known to you why his hand is not removed from you. Then said they, What shall be the trespass offering which we shall return to him? They answered, Five golden emerods, and five golden mice, according to the number of the lords of the Philistines: for one plague was on you all, and on your lords. Therefore ye shall make images of your emerods, and images of your mice that mar the land; and ye shall give glory unto the God of Israel: peradventure he will lighten his hand from off you, and from off your gods, and from off your land. Wherefore then do ye harden your hearts, as the Egyptians and Pharaoh hardened their hearts? when he had wrought wonderfully among them, did they not let the people go, and they departed?

"Now therefore make a new cart, and take two milch kine [milk cows], on which there hath come no yoke, and tie the kine to the cart, and bring their calves home from them: And take the ark of the LORD, and lay it upon the cart; and put the jewels of gold, which ye return him for a trespass offering, in a coffer by the side thereof; and send it away, that it may go. And see, if it goeth up by the way of his own coast to Bethshemesh, then he hath done us this great evil: but if not, then we shall know that it is not his hand that smote us: it was a chance that happened to us. And the men did so; and took two milch kine, and tied them to the cart, and shut up their calves at home: And they laid the ark of the LORD upon the cart, and the coffer with the mice of gold and the images of their emerods. And the kine took the straight way to the way of Bethshemesh, and went along the highway, lowing as they went, and turned not aside to the right hand or to the left; and the lords of the Philistines went after them unto the border of Bethshemesh" (I Samuel 6:1–12).

The diviners in this passage were those who had religious understanding. Their solution included harnessing two nursing cows to a new cart and watching to see if they would supernaturally leave their calves and return the cart to Israel on their own accord.

Years later, David attempted to bring this ark from Kirjathjearim into the capital city: "And David consulted with the captains of thousands and hundreds, and with every leader. And David said unto all the congregation of Israel, If it seem good unto you, and that it be of the LORD our God, let us send abroad unto our brethren every where, that are left in all the land of Israel, and with them also to the priests and Levites which are in their cities and suburbs, that they may gather themselves unto us: And let us bring again the ark of our God to us: for we enquired not at it in the days of Saul. And all the congregation said that they would do so: for the thing was right in the eyes of all the people.

"So David gathered all Israel together, from Shihor of Egypt even unto the entering of Hemath, to bring the ark of God from Kirjathjearim. And David went up, and all Israel, to Baalah, that is, to Kirjathjearim, which belonged to Judah, to bring up thence the ark of God the LORD, that dwelleth between the cherubims. . . . And they carried the ark of God in a new cart out of the house of Abinadab: and Uzza and Ahio drave the cart. And David and all Israel played before God with all their might, and with singing, and with harps, and with psalteries, and with timbrels, and with cymbals, and with trumpets. And when they came unto the threshingfloor of Chidon, Uzza put forth his hand to hold the ark; for the oxen stumbled. And the anger of the LORD was kindled against Uzza, and he smote him, because he put his hand to the ark: and there he died before God. And David was displeased, because the LORD had made a breach upon Uzza: wherefore that place is called Perezuzza to this day. And David was afraid of God that day, saying, How shall I bring the ark of God home to me? So David brought not the ark home to himself to the city of David, but carried it aside into the house of Obededom the Gittite. And the ark of God remained with the family of Obededom in his house

> There are serious consequences to the methods we employ in doing good works for the Lord.

three months. And the Lord blessed the house of Obededom, and all that he had" (I Chronicles 13:1–14).

There is no reason to doubt David's sincerity and motives before God. The problem existed in the method David chose to do a good thing. He put the ark of God in a new cart just as the Philistines had done. He imitated the ways of the world. Just because something is new does not necessarily make it better. The results in this case were disastrous: one man was killed, David became displeased and afraid of God, and the huge procession came to a discouraging halt.

A universal Biblical truth revealed in these passages is that there are serious consequences to the methods we employ in doing good works for the Lord. The end does not justify the means! God tolerated this illegitimate method for the heathen, but He rejected it for His own people.

What did David do following this disaster? He did what any man of God would do following a failure. He repented, went back to the Scriptures, and learned how to do God's work after the due order. God is a God of order: "And David called for Zadok and Abiathar the priests, and for the Levites, for Uriel, Asaiah, and Joel, Shemaiah, and Eliel, and Amminadab, and said unto them, Ye are the chief of the fathers of the Levites: sanctify yourselves, both ye and your brethren, that ye may bring up the ark of the Lord God of Israel unto the place that I have prepared for it. For because ye did it not at the first, the Lord our God made a breach upon us, for that we sought him not after the due order. So the priests and the Levites sanctified

> The end does not justify the means!

themselves to bring up the ark of the LORD God of Israel. And the children of the Levites bare the ark of God upon their shoulders with the staves thereon, as Moses commanded according to the word of the LORD" (I Chronicles 15:11–15, based on Numbers 7:1–9).

Worldly methods, including worldly musical forms, cannot be used to carry out holy works, such as preaching God's Word: "And if a man also strive for masteries, yet is he not crowned, except he strive lawfully" (II Timothy 2:5). Fanny Crosby said, "The church must never sing its songs to the melodies of the world." [1]

Imitation is a form of admiration, and God will never tolerate it when His people imitate the ways of the world. (See I John 2:15–16.) For Christians to imitate the music styles of the world is to openly show how much they inwardly admire the world: "They did not destroy the nations, concerning whom the LORD commanded them: But were mingled among the heathen, and learned their works" (Psalm 106:34–35). We must constantly guard our hearts from the attraction of worldly methods: "Wherefore come out from among them, and be ye separate, saith the Lord, and touch not the unclean thing; and I will receive you, and will be a Father unto you, and ye shall be my sons and daughters, saith the Lord Almighty" (II Corinthians 6:17–18).

2. DO NOT MIX THE CLEAN WITH THE UNCLEAN

Let's consider the Biblical principles that describe the relationship between that which is clean and that which is unclean, as spoken by the Word of the LORD through the prophet Haggai. The purpose of God's message to Haggai was to arouse the people to return to the work of rebuilding the temple, which had been suspended through their disobedience. The altar that had been built earlier under Cyrus was left exposed in the open air. (See Ezra 3:3–7.)

Notice how Haggai now motivates the people by referring to a section of the ceremonial law and applies the principle within that law to the work of rebuilding: "Thus saith the

> Haggai motivated the people by applying the principle within a section of the ceremonial law to the work of rebuilding.

Lord of hosts; Ask now the priests concerning the law, saying, If one bear holy flesh in the skirt of his garment, and with his skirt do touch bread, or pottage, or wine, or oil, or any meat, shall it be holy? And the priests answered and said, No" (Haggai 2:11–12).

The *holy flesh*, or sacrificial offering, is a symbol of Christ. (See I Corinthians 5:7.) The *skirt* represents that which carries holy flesh—the means God may use to communicate Christ. Because this vessel was in direct contact with the sacrifice, it was also holy. (See Leviticus 6:27.) The common items touched by the skirt represent anything unclean. This refers to that which is worldly and outside of Christ even though it may be socially acceptable.

One of the means (pictured as a skirt) God used to communicate divine truth about Christ in the Old Testament was the ceremonial offerings, which the people were dutifully offering. The question that God and Haggai are getting to is this: Can the means of the ceremonial offerings make the common people holy and acceptable to God if the people themselves were not in direct contact and fellowship with Christ because of their disobedience? The answer is no. No matter how faithful they were to the ceremony, the ceremonial means could not make them acceptable to God.

To become acceptable to God they needed to come into direct contact with God and have a change of heart, as evidenced by obeying His direction to rebuild: "For thou desirest not sacrifice; else would I give it: thou delightest not in burnt offering. The sacrifices of God are a broken spirit: a broken and a contrite heart, O God, thou wilt not despise" (Psalm 51:16–17).

> The means God uses to communicate truth cannot in and of itself impart holiness to anything.

Consider how this universal principle applies to preaching. Christ gives a sermon to a preacher who delivers it to an audience. The sermon and the preacher may be pictured as the means or vessels through which Christ desires to communicate truth and impart His life. Can the sermon itself make the people in the audience holy? There is influence in the means God uses, but there is no inherent power in the means itself to make unholy people holy: "For unto us was the gospel preached, as well as unto them: but the word preached did not profit them, not being mixed with faith in them that heard it" (Hebrews 4:2). When the message preached to the unholy was mixed with faith that brought them into direct contact with Christ Himself, then that which was unholy was changed by Christ Himself and made holy.

The means God uses to communicate truth cannot in and of itself impart holiness to anything. For the thing to become holy it must be changed and conformed to Christ: "I beseech you therefore, brethren, by the mercies of God, that ye present your bodies a living sacrifice, holy, acceptable unto God, which is your reasonable service. And be not conformed to this world: but be ye transformed by the renewing of your mind, that ye may prove what is that good, and acceptable, and perfect, will of God" (Romans 12:1–2). To present our bodies as a sacrifice to Christ, Who is our Sacrifice, is to die daily with Him. (See Luke 9:23.) The beauty of this sacrifice is that it is a living sacrifice by which He lives His resurrected life through us. (See Romans 6:5 and Galatians 2:20.) It is His holy life in us that makes us holy, acceptable to God. The more a believer is conformed to Christ, the less he will be conformed to the world; the less will be his desire to imitate the world because of the transforming (changing) power of Christ.

Consider how this universal principle applies to music. Another means that God uses to communicate truth is music. Consider an acceptable piece of music that is sung with unholy lyrics of lust and violence. We may be able to block out the vile words and to enjoy the music, but can the holy music make holy those unholy words, which are outside of God's nature and contrary to His truth? If you say no, then you are in agreement with the priests of Haggai's day. For those words to become holy, they must be brought into direct contact with Christ and be changed to reflect His divine truth.

In the same way, consider a situation in which acceptable lyrics are sung with worldly music. We are able to block out the vile music and enjoy the words, but can the holy words make holy the unholy music, which is outside of God's nature and contrary to His truth? Again, no. For that music to become holy, it must be brought into direct contact with Christ and be changed to reflect His divine nature.

After establishing that holy things cannot of themselves change unholy things, Haggai poses a second question to warn about the danger of what unholy things can do: "Then said Haggai, If one that is unclean by a dead body touch any of these, shall it be unclean? And the priests answered and said, It shall be unclean" (Haggai 2:13).

In this second scenario, the ones who are unholy (unclean because of contact with a dead body) are the people to whom Haggai is speaking. In this context, the people are the vessels as they dutifully fulfilled their religious ceremonies. However, the people are unclean because of their direct contact with a dead body, which is symbolic of death, evil, or Satan. They are not in direct contact with God, as evidenced by their disobedient hearts in neglecting His will to rebuild the temple. The things they were touching were the very offerings they were presenting in their hands.

> A little worldly beat can defile many godly words . . .

Here, the question that God and Haggai are getting to is this: If the people are in direct contact with evil, as indicated by their disobedience and neglect to rebuild, can their means of following correct ceremonial procedures make their offerings holy and acceptable to God? Again, the answer is no. Because their hearts were not in harmony with God, the very offerings they touched, though normally acceptable, were made unclean and unacceptable to God.

The principle behind this teaching is that impurity is more readily communicated than purity. The paths to sin are manifold; there is a single path to holiness. One drop of filth will defile a vase of water; many drops of water will not purify a vase of filth. One bad apple will spoil the barrel, so don't mix them.

In regard to preaching, one false teacher can lead many astray. One person with a root of bitterness can defile many who are not close enough to Christ to draw on His power to overcome it: "Looking diligently lest any man fail of the grace of God; lest any root of bitterness springing up trouble you, and thereby many be defiled" (Hebrews 12:15).

In regard to music, a little worldly beat can defile many godly words by communicating to the young, the weak, and the unsuspecting the unholy message that you can be a Christian and still "do what you want to do." A little leaven is dangerous, so periodically Israel observed the Feast of Unleavened Bread to remove this symbol of sin from their midst.

Ungodly music should not be tolerated. To mix ungodly music with godly words is to be like the double-minded children of Israel when they were delivered into the hands of the Assyrians: "They feared the LORD, and served their own gods, after the manner of the nations [who carried them away from thence]" (II Kings 17:33).

3. SOW TO THE SPIRIT NOT TO THE FLESH

One way to evaluate melody, harmony, and rhythm is to relate them to the three parts of our being. We are primarily a spirit, with a soul, in a physical body: "And the very God of peace sanctify you wholly; and I pray God your whole spirit and soul and body be preserved blameless unto the coming of our Lord Jesus Christ" (I Thessalonians 5:23).

Our spirit is the new nature that is born again and is in direct relationship with God. Our spirit includes our God consciousness, Christlike behavior, and communion with the Holy Spirit. We must be born again in our spirit. (See John 3:6–7.) If the tabernacle is a picture of our being, then the Holy of Holies would be a picture of our spirit, in which we have fellowship with the Father through the blood of Christ. (See Hebrews 10:19.)

Our soul includes our capacity to reason, our wide range of emotions, our capacity to make decisions, and our unique personality traits. The Inner Court would be a picture of our soul, which has fellowship with others who are gathered with us in worship.

Our body includes our five physical senses, and it provides the underlying support for our soul and spirit to function in this physical world. The Outer Court would be a picture of our body, which is the outward expression of our being.

> It is the rise in the melody that provides the primary capacity for music to raise our spirits upward to God.

As we analyze melody, harmony, and rhythm individually, consider how the melody relates to our spirit, the harmony relates to our soul, and the rhythm relates to our body. Which part of our being is the most important part? Which part should be the most dominant if we want God's best for our lives and His kingdom?

Melody

Melody is primarily associated with our spirit. It is the rise in the melody that provides the primary capacity for music to raise our spirits upward to God. Other parts of music can affect our spirit, but by definition, it is the melody that lifts the music and thus it is primarily the melody that provides the climax for the high point in music.

The Greek word for *melody* is *psallo* [#5567]. It occurs four times in the New Testament, and each time it is associated with our spirit:

- Ephesians 5:18–19: "And be not drunk with wine, wherein is excess; but be filled with the Spirit; speaking to yourselves in psalms and hymns and spiritual songs, singing and making melody [*psallo*] in your heart to the Lord." Here is a direct association of melody with the filling of the Holy Spirit in our innermost being.

- Romans 15:9: "And that the Gentiles might glorify God for his mercy; as it is written, For this cause I will confess to thee among the Gentiles, and sing [*psallo*] unto thy name." In this passage, the singing is a joining in with the Gentiles on a spiritual level as they glorify God, independent of their different nationalities. (See also I Corinthians 6:20.)

- I Corinthians 14:15: "What is it then? I will pray with the spirit, and I will pray with the understanding also: I will sing [*psallo*] with the spirit, and I will sing with the understanding also." This is another direct association of the melody with our spirit.

- James 5:13: "Is any among you afflicted? let him pray. Is any merry? let him sing [*psallo*] psalms." Here again, the singing is an expression of a cheerful heart of joy, which is a fruit of the Spirit (Galatians 5:22–23). As individuals depart from a congregation that has been singing, it is primarily the melody and not the harmony or rhythm that goes with them. The message of the song is more easily remembered as we hum the melody.

Harmony

Harmony is primarily associated with our soul. Harmony occurs when a group of individual notes are played simultaneously together. The emphasis is not on the rise and fall but on the relationship of the individual notes with each other. These groups of notes are called chords.

When the individual souls of the New Testament church were in harmony with each other, they were said to be in "one accord," as in one chord: "And they, continuing daily with one accord in the temple, and breaking bread from house to house, did eat their meat with gladness and singleness of heart" (Acts 2:46).

> When the individual souls of the New Testament church were in harmony with each other, they were said to be in "one accord," as in one chord . . .

Whereas the melody relates to our personal relationship with God, the harmony in music is associated with our social relationship with other members of the Body of Christ. In music that is consistent with

God's nature, the harmony will be supportive of the melody and play a subservient, though critical, role.

Rhythm

Rhythm is associated with our body. There are many rhythms in our bodies, such as patterns in brain waves, breathing, and heartbeats. Every single cell in our skeleton is replaced according to a seven-year cycle. [2]

In God's wisdom we need to keep our body under subjection: "But I keep under my body, and bring it into subjection: lest that by any means, when I have preached to others, I myself should be a castaway" (I Corinthians 9:27). This is because sin so casily enters our lives through our physical drives: "Let not sin therefore reign in your mortal body, that ye should obey it in the lusts thereof" (Romans 6:12).

Recall that it is the rhythm that can easily incite the flesh and lower restraint and self-control. Therefore the rhythm, like our bodies, must be "kept under," concealed, and brought into the subjection of strict control.

A spiritual person whose life is in balance and in order will have a dominant spirit, a wholesome soul, and a supportive body. A carnal person whose life is out of balance will have a dominant focus on his body, conflicts in his soul, and little interest in spiritual things.

Therefore, godly music, which is in balance and in order, will have a dominant melody, a wholesome harmony, and a supportive rhythm. Worldly music, which is out of balance and disorderly, will have a dominant rhythm, discord in the harmony, and a suppressed melody.

Does the type of music you listen to reflect these three aspects of our being in a godly way or in a carnal way? Note that Paul is speaking to Christians when he says, "That ye put off concerning the former conversation the old man, which is corrupt according to the deceitful lusts; and be renewed in the spirit of your mind; and that ye put on the new man, which after God is created in righteousness and true holiness" (Ephesians 4:22–24). "For he that soweth to his flesh shall of the flesh reap corruption; but he that soweth to the Spirit shall of the Spirit reap life everlasting" (Galatians 6:8).

Based on the First Commandment, we should always seek God's best: "And thou shalt love the Lord thy God with all thy heart, and with all thy soul, and with all thy mind, and with all thy strength: this is the first commandment" (Mark 12:30). If we really want God's best in music, let's not seek a line separating "good" and "bad," but rather let us seek to establish a gap, a clear difference between the holy and the unholy, between the clean and the unclean, between the spiritual and the carnal, between the Christlike and the worldly.

> If we invite someone to church who has come out of a worldly lifestyle, do we want him to hear church music that arouses his old passions?

The following commands in Scripture compel us not to "draw a line" of separation from evil but rather to create a gap between good and evil: "Abstain from all appearance of evil" (I Thessalonians 5:22). "But put ye on the Lord Jesus Christ, and make not provision for the flesh, to fulfill the lusts thereof" (Romans 13:14).

If we invite someone to church who has come out of a worldly lifestyle, do we want him to hear church music that arouses his old passions? Do we want him to get the message that he can be a Christian and be sensual at the same time? Do we want to give him one message with our words and another with our music?

Are you willing to take a stand for righteousness in regard to music, in order to avoid all appearance of an acceptance of worldly music?

ENDNOTES: SECTION II

Chapter 4

1 www.earlymusic.dikmans.net/quotes.html. (Quoted in Shapiro, *An Encyclopedia of Quotations about Music*, 1978.)

2 www.toddgreen.com/quotes.html

3 www.a-voice.org/main/voice021.htm

4 www.brainyquote.com/quotes/keywords/degrades.html

5 www.reversespins.com/music.html

6 William Kilpatrick, Professor of Education, Boston College, *Why Johnny Can't Tell Right From Wrong*, pp. 178, 182

7 www.catholiceducation.org/articles/education/ed0081.html

8 David Noebel in *The Legacy of John Lennon*

9 *Time*, October 31, 1969, p. 49

10 www.insiderockmusic.com/destroy.html

11 *How to Conquer the Addiction of Rock Music*, p. 23

12 Steve Lawhead in his writing, *Rock Reconsidered*

13 Research paper titled "Hear That Long Snake Moan" by Michael Ventura in the *Whole Earth Review*, Spring 1987, pp. 28–43, and Summer 1987, pp. 82–92

14 David Tame, *The Secret Power of Music*, p. 199

15 *Solomon's Secret*, Multnomah Press, 1985, p. 10

Chapter 5

1 www.andras-nagy.com/AcceleratedLearning/07.htm

2 www.en.wikipedia.org/wiki/Cymatics

3 www.thefreedictionary.com/chord

4 www.en.wikipedia.org/wiki/Garden_Party_(Rick_Nelson_song)

5 Mickey Hart, drummer for the Grateful Dead, *Drumming at the Edge of Magic*, pp. 64, 209–212

6 Steve Turner, *Hungry for Heaven*, p. 26

7 www.en.wikipedia.org/wiki/B-boying

8 www.vnnforum.com/showthread.php?p=1032930

9 www.conservapedia.com/Rock

10 www.tools-for-abundance.com/hypnosis.html

11 www.esensuality.com/sensual-tips/how-to-give-lap-dance.php

Chapter 6

1 www.discerningmusic.wordpress.com/random-music-quotes

2 www.stemcell.stanford.edu/research

SECTION III

A History of Music

SECTION III WILL LOOK AT the history of music from three perspectives. In Chapter 7 we look at the history of music through the testimonies of Scripture. In Chapter 8 we look at the history of African tribal music from the perspective of the Garden of Eden and see how that music has spread to the American culture. Finally, in Chapter 9 we will look at the dangerous influence of New Age philosophies in contemporary music.

A Prayer for God's Perspective

Lord, help us to do as You commanded in Deuteronomy 32:7–8: "Remember the days of old, consider the years of many generations: ask thy father, and he will shew thee; thy elders, and they will tell thee. When the most High divided to the nations their inheritance, when he separated the sons of Adam . . . ."

CHAPTER 7

A Biblical History of Music

THIS CHAPTER IS NOT INTENDED to be a thorough study of every reference to music in Scripture. Rather, it is a chronological overview of some of the significant times when music is mentioned in the Bible, especially within the context of worship services. The following five points highlight some important insights that God has revealed about music.

1. MUSIC IS NOT REQUIRED FOR WORSHIP

Although not specifically stated in Scripture, it is very likely that Adam worshipped God. We do know that Cain and Abel worshipped the LORD with their offerings: "And in process of time it came to pass, that Cain brought of the fruit of the ground an offering unto the LORD. And Abel, he also brought of the first-lings of his flock and of the fat thereof. And the LORD had respect unto Abel and to his offering. But unto Cain and to his offering he had not respect. And Cain was very wroth, and his countenance fell" (Genesis 4:3–5). Clearly God had requirements for acceptable worship, but there is no mention of music as a requirement.

As a matter of fact, the first mention of any type of music in the Bible does not occur until six generations after Cain:

"And his brother's name *was* Jubal: he was the father of all such as handle the harp and organ" (Genesis 4:21). Because Jubal was the father of all such that handled musical instruments, the clear implication is that there were no musical instruments used in worship prior to that time. If there was any singing at this time it is not mentioned in Scripture as a requirement for worship.

When God gave detailed instructions to Moses about the construction of the Tabernacle, which was to be the center of worship for Israel, He did not establish a single provision regarding the use of music in those public services. (See Exodus 25–27.) Music may be a genuine result of true fellowship with the Lord and a meaningful *part* of a worship service, but it certainly is not a *requirement* for a worship service.

> Clearly God had requirements for acceptable worship, but there is no mention of music as a requirement.

Perhaps some church congregations should experiment with a worship service *in spirit and in truth* without any music. If this is found to be "unfulfilling," then it should raise a suspicion of the possibility that an emotional addiction has become intermingled with true worship.

Also, based on the definition of the word *worship*, it is evident that music is not required for worship. The Hebrew word for *worship* is *shachah* [#7812], which means to "bow down" (as in homage to royalty or God); to "do reverence"; to "humbly beseech."

The first mention of "worship" in the Bible is in connection with Abraham, and this Hebrew word is translated *bowed*:

"And he lift up his eyes and looked, and, lo, three men stood by him: and when he saw *them,* he ran to meet them from the tent door, and bowed [#7812] himself toward the ground" (Genesis 18:2). The primary characteristic of worship is humility, which includes submission, surrender, examination, confession, and sacrifice. "The sacrifices of God *are* a broken spirit: a broken and a contrite heart, O God, thou wilt not despise" (Psalm 51:17).

Music should be appropriate for the occasion. For example, it would not be appropriate to play rousing march music at a funeral where a family is grieving: "Rejoice with them that do rejoice, and weep with them that weep" (Romans 12:15). In the same way music that is appropriate for praise would not be appropriate for worship because praise and worship are not synonymous.

One of the most common words for praise in the Old Testament is *yadah* [#3034], which means "to hold out the hand." Another common Old Testament word is halal [#1984], which means "to celebrate." The New Testament also associates praise with joy and celebration: ". . . the whole multitude of the disciples began to rejoice and praise God with a loud voice for all the mighty works that they had seen" (Luke 19:37). Praise and worship are similar in that both are done in reverence and honor to God, but technically they are different. Praise includes lifting up the hands in a reverent spirit of rejoicing while worship involves bowing down in a reverent spirit of brokenness. A church service may include

> Praise and worship are similar in that both are done in reverence and honor to God, but they are different.

both praise and worship, but they are not the same. And if music is used with each, the style of music should be appropriate for each. However, there is no indication in Scripture that music is required for either, and there is no Biblical basis for music to take center stage the way it has in so many "worship services."

A danger associated with many Contemporary Christian Music services is that the praise music tends to override the worship music. This is so because it is more natural to embrace rejoicing than it is to embrace suffering. It is more natural to celebrate than to confess. It is more natural to lift oneself up than it is to bow oneself down. However, a true worship service in spirit and in truth includes both. Listen to the heart of a mature church leader: "That I may know Him, and the power of his resurrection [celebration and praise], and the fellowship of his sufferings [brokenness and worship], being made conformable unto his death" (Philippians 3:10).

> "David introduced music into public worship on his own initiative."

In this book we will use the phrase *worship service* when referring in a general way to all the components of a public gathering of believers, including praise, worship, preaching, prayer, etc.

2. MUSIC IS PERMITTED IN WORSHIP SERVICES

There is no indication in the Bible that music was a regular part of public worship services in Israel until the time of David: "And these are they whom David set over the service of song in the house of the LORD, after that the ark had rest" (I Chronicles 6:31).

This verse and the following passages indicate that David introduced music into public worship on his own initiative.

- "Moreover four thousand were porters; and four thousand praised the LORD with the instruments which I made, said David, to praise therewith" (I Chronicles 23:5).

- At the dedication of the rebuilding of the wall around Jerusalem certain of the priests' sons came ". . . with the musical instruments of David the man of God . . ." (Nehemiah 12:36).

- In a time of apostasy Israel was defending their luxurious passion for music by stating that they could "invent to themselves instruments of music, like David" (Amos 6:5). This passage will be explained further in the following point: "Music Must Be Used With Caution."

There is no indication in Scripture that God ever gave any direct revelation to David to institute this service of song. Neither is there any indication in Scripture that God rebuked David for doing so. Thus, music is permitted in public worship as a joyous expression of the Spirit.

Even though the words of the Psalms were inspired and were declared for the glory of God, David added music to public worship in the Tabernacle on his own initiative. All Biblical references to David's introduction of music into the worship service indicate that it was by permission, not by express command.

Music may be the result of a meaningful relationship with God, as it was with David. Praise and worship music are welcome additions to a worship service and may even be present on a regular basis, but we should never base the success of a worship service on the presence or absence of music. Music should never become an idol that is exalted to a position of greater importance than the teaching of doctrine and other elements of worship services such as fellowship, communion, or prayer. (See Acts 2:42.)

God did not say that His house would be called a house of music but rather a house of prayer: "Even them will I bring to my holy mountain, and make them joyful in my house of prayer: their burnt offerings and their sacrifices shall be accepted upon mine altar; for mine house shall be called an house of prayer for all people" (Isaiah 56:7). Jesus confirmed this definition. (See Matthew 21:13.) David's Psalms are referred to as prayers: "The prayers of David the son of Jesse are ended" (Psalm 72:20). The emotional messages in the music should support the verbal messages in the worship service, not dominate them.

> God did not say that His house would be called a house of music but rather a house of prayer.

Although music communicates a powerful message, God's primary means of revealing Himself and communicating truth is through His Word: "To the law and to the testimony: if they speak not according to this word, it is because there is no light in them" (Isaiah 8:20; see also I Corinthians 1:21).

3. MUSIC MUST BE USED WITH CAUTION

The following analysis of Amos 5:1 through 6:6 confirms the need for caution against a self-indulgent lifestyle that includes careless self-expression in music. Insights on the historical background for these verses are from the *Jamieson, Fausset, and Brown Commentary on the Whole Bible.*

One of the things Amos rebuked Israel for in a time of apostasy was their excessive passion for music. During a time of carelessness and carnality in their worship services, God sent His *word* to Israel through the prophet Amos: "Hear ye this word which I take up against you, *even* a lamentation, O house of Israel" (Amos 5:1). The Hebrew word for *lamentation* [#7015] refers to a dirge or mourning accompanied by beating the breast in heartfelt grief.

In verses 2 through 20 Amos speaks rebuke to God's people for being slack in regard to practicing righteousness: "Ye who turn judgment to wormwood, and leave off righteousness in the earth" (Amos 5:7). The Hebrew word for the phrase *leave off* [#3240] is *yawnakh*, which means to "leave alone" or "lay off." God was grieved that His people had let go of their righteous standard and had become careless spiritually. Their lives, including their music as will be seen shortly, were being guided by subjective personal preferences and not according to objective righteous principles.

In verses 14–15 Amos calls for a change, but knowing that brokenness is not forthcoming, God says, "I hate, I despise your feast days, and I will not smell in your solemn assemblies" (Amos 5:21). Their feast days were their worship services, yet God despised the practices they had embraced as a means of worship: "Though ye offer me burnt offerings and your meat offerings, I will not accept them: neither will I regard the peace offerings of your fat beasts. Take thou away from me the noise of thy songs; for I will not hear the melody of thy viols" (Amos 5:22–23).

Why did God not want to hear their songs? God rejected them because they were not sung in spirit and in truth. God is not pleased with any part of a worship service that is inconsistent with His holy nature, including the music.

What did God want? "But let judgment run down as waters, and righteousness as a mighty stream" (Amos 5:24). It is important that we judge ourselves, "for if we would judge ourselves, we should not be judged. But when we are judged, we are chastened of the Lord, that we should not be condemned with the world" (I Corinthians 11:31–32). We must judge ourselves and our music in order to eliminate all worldly influences from our lives so that we will not be condemned with the world.

> We must judge ourselves and our music . . . so that we will not be condemned with the world.

Amos then gives an example of their compromise in mixing worldly elements with their worship services: "Have ye offered unto me sacrifices and offerings in the wilderness forty years, O house of Israel? But ye have borne the tabernacle of your Moloch and Chiun your images, the star of your god, which ye made to yourselves" (Amos 5:25–26). The tabernacles of Moloch and Chiun were images hidden among their personal possessions that were small enough to have been carried forty years through the desert without being detected by Moses. Note that God did not tell Amos to "reach" His people and get their attention with music but rather by warning them to practice judgment and righteousness and to turn from mocking God with mixed worship. They were mixing devotion to God with devotion to idols. Likewise, we must not mix godly words with worldly music.

"Therefore will I cause you to go into captivity beyond Damascus, saith the LORD, whose name is The God of hosts" (Amos 5:27). God is sending them into captivity, not primarily because of sins we would judge as vile today such as violence, pornography, abortion, or sodomy, but because of mixed worship. They were not loving God with all their heart in ways that were pleasing Him, and they were compromising their worship services in ways that were pleasing to themselves.

"Woe to them that are at ease in Zion, and trust in the mountain of Samaria, which are named chief of the nations, to whom the house of Israel came!" (Amos 6:1). They were at ease; they thought they were safe; they thought they were okay with God, and yet there was an obvious lack of the power of God in their lives and in their nation. They were falsely resting on past accomplishments, such as the seizure of the mountain of Samaria, a stronghold that was overcome when Israel first entered Canaan.

"Pass ye unto Calneh, and see; and from thence go ye to Hamath the great: then go down to Gath of the Philistines: be they better than these kingdoms? or their border greater than your border?" (Amos 6:2). In God's judgment all these pagan cities had recently been conquered. And in God's mercies, Israel, who was acting no differently than those whom God had just judged and cast out, was temporarily spared. Israel had no more reason than these cities to expect exemption from the consequences of their sins. Amos's warning was that just as these cities had been punished, so would Israel's cities be punished.

Why, then, would Israel imitate them? How vain was Israel's imagined confidence in their perceived safety: "Ye that put far away the evil day, and cause the seat of violence to come near" (Amos 6:3). They put far away the evil day in their imagination. The notion of judgment being far off or being escaped altogether has always been an incentive to embrace reckless living.

In an attempt to waken His people to the seriousness of their carnal state, Amos presents a convincing list of their excessive worldly ways:

- "That lie upon beds of ivory, and stretch themselves upon their couches, and eat the lambs out of the flock, and the calves out of the midst of the stall" (Amos 6:4). Beds of ivory speak of luxurious self-indulgence. The lambs and calves were picked out as the choicest, for their selfish gratification.

- "That chant to the sound of the viol, and invent to themselves instruments of music, like David" (Amos 6:5). Here is another reference to music in this time of apostasy. To chant [#6527] is to scatter words. In the context of these other self-centered behaviors, it would include carelessness in music. They were defending their luxurious passion for music by referring to David's use of music, forgetting that David pursued his study of music from a delight in God's Word that found expression in praise, not from a delight in entertainment for an emotional high.

- "That drink wine in bowls, and anoint themselves with the chief ointments: but they are not grieved for the affliction of Joseph" (Amos 6:6). Drinking out of bowls reveals lack of satisfaction with the smaller cups, which were normally used. Chief ointments were not just ointments for health or cleanliness but were the most costly—wanton luxury. A lack of self-control leads to insensitivity to the need for total surrender to God, insensitivity to the absence of His blessing, and insensitivity to the nearness of judgment. The example Amos gives is their forefathers, the sons of Jacob, who showed such insensitivity toward Joseph that they were able to eat bread while their brother lay in the pit and then sell him into slavery to the Ishmaelites. (See Genesis 37:25.)

Historically, Israel had become careless and carnal (see Amos 5:7) in their worship services, and they defended their luxurious passion for music (see Amos 6:5) by referring to what David had added to the worship services. However, they went beyond David's liberty into license and lack of restraint. "For, brethren, ye have been called unto liberty; only use not liberty for an occasion to the flesh, but by love serve one another" (Galatians 5:13).

They were wrong in their justification, and God sent Amos to correct them. They were wrong in what they were adding, because what they were adding was false and inconsistent with God's nature, as evidenced by the focus on their musical chant (see Amos 6:5) and on their personal pleasures (see Amos 6:4–6).

What David added to the public worship service was acceptable to God, because what he added was true and consistent with God's nature. We can add godly music to our worship services, but we must use great caution not to mix unclean musical elements with holy, spiritual music from the heart of God. Israel was perverting music for their own gratification, for entertainment, and for personal fulfillment. Note that Israel was doing all this at a time when God was ready to bring judgment upon them.

4. MUSIC LEADERS MUST BE APPROVED

Because music is the language of the emotions, an emotional experience can easily become confused with a spiritual experience. When this occurs, we can come to the point of worshipping our praise and praising our worship.

Bible study is needed to clearly distinguish even good emotional experience from true spiritual experience. Care must be taken in the use of music during worship because of how easily it can be taken to excess and how tempting it is to exalt emotional experience over spiritual experience.

What guidance is available to equip us to avoid this confusion and to develop needed spiritual discernment? That guidance is the Word of God, which is "quick, and powerful, and sharper than any two-edged sword, piercing even to the dividing asunder of soul [including the human emotions] and spirit, and of the joints and marrow, and is a discerner of the thoughts and intents of the heart" (Hebrews 4:12).

The specific Biblical guidance that God gives to discern emotional experience from spiritual experience occurs at a point in time when music was first introduced in public worship. When David made music a part of public worship, note those who were selected as the singers: "And David spake to the chief of the Levites to appoint their brethren to be the singers with instruments of music, psalteries and harps and cymbals, sounding, by lifting up the voice with joy" (I Chronicles 15:16).

The Levites were those in Israel who were especially dedicated to the Lord. They received additional training in the law, and they were the teachers of the law and the holy ways of God. With these individuals performing the music, there would be an extra level of protection in detecting and avoiding anything that would be contrary to the law and God's nature. The Levites would be the ones most capable of "proving what is acceptable unto the Lord" (Ephesians 5:10).

There needs to be a process of proving those who lead music in worship services, just as we have a process of proving those who proclaim the Word in worship services. Natural speaking abilities or musical skills are of secondary importance. Scripture holds spiritual leaders to a high moral standard: "If any be blameless, the husband of one wife, having faithful children not accused of riot or unruly. For a bishop [spiritual leader] must be blameless, as the steward of God; not self-willed, not soon angry, not given to wine, no striker, not given to filthy lucre; but a lover of hospitality, a lover of good men, sober, just, holy, temperate" (Titus 1:6–8). Thus, God's standard includes mature character that is gained by obedience to a holy God. God's standard also requires a leader to faithfully follow the Scripture and to effectively persuade others to do so: "Holding fast the faithful word as he hath been taught, that he may be

> When David made music a part of public worship, note those who were selected as the singers.

able by sound doctrine both to exhort and to convince the gain-sayers" (Titus 1:9). A godly lifestyle that is founded on the truth of God's Word will provide the spiritual discernment that is needed to distinguish that which is in the flesh (emotional only) from that which is in the Spirit. Without a predetermined standard, an unspoken and untested axiom that will fail to shield God's people from the lie that music is amoral and that any type of music is acceptable will surface in the Church.

One passage of Scripture may, at first glance, imply that God commanded David to institute his service in song. Years after David's reign, Israel turned away from the Lord. Good king Hezekiah instituted reforms to cleanse the house of God: "And he [Hezekiah] set the Levites in the house of the LORD with cymbals, with psalteries, and with harps, according to the commandment of David, and of Gad the king's seer, and Nathan the prophet: for so was the commandment of the LORD by his prophets" (II Chronicles 29:25).

> David was permitted to add music to public worship, but the Levites were commanded to perform it.

However, note the following analysis of this verse from *Adam Clarke's Bible Commentary*: "It was by the hand or commandment of the LORD and his prophets that the Levites should praise the LORD; for so the Hebrew text may be understood: and it was by the order of David that so many instruments of music should be introduced into the Divine service."

Thus, what God commanded was not that David should introduce music into worship but rather that the Levites were to be the ones to lead music. David was permitted to add music to public worship, but the Levites were commanded to perform it. The Levites were those trained in the law and the ways of God. If churches violate this Biblical direction and permit untested music leaders to exercise authority during worship services, they run the risk of misrepresenting the nature of God and promoting carnal behavior.

The commandment that the Levites were to lead the music (see I Chronicles 15:16) is consistent with the musical nature of God. In Chapter 2 it was demonstrated that music has the power to communicate moral messages in the same way that words do. Care must be taken to ensure that these messages are consistent with God's nature, and God gives this responsibility and authority primarily to mature, spiritual leaders.

5. LACK OF MATURITY IN MUSICAL PERFORMERS WILL HAVE CONSEQUENCES

Division and confusion are to be expected if music is evaluated on the basis of subjective personal preferences and not on the basis of objective Biblical truth.

The first occurrence in the Bible of the English word *music* (spelled *musick* in the King James Version) is within a description of an occasion on which music was sung with sincerity in celebration. However, the music was not sung with the oversight of mature leadership, and the result was sharp division: "And David went out whithersoever Saul sent him, and behaved himself wisely: and Saul set him over the men of war, and he was accepted in the sight of all the people, and also in the sight of Saul's servants. And it came to pass as they came, when David was returned from the slaughter of the Philistine, that the women came out of all cities of Israel, singing and dancing, to meet king Saul, with tabrets, with joy, and with instruments of musick. And the women answered one another as they played, and said, Saul hath slain his thousands, and David his ten thousands. And Saul was very wroth, and the saying displeased him; and he said, They have ascribed unto David ten thousands, and to me they have ascribed but thousands: and what can he have more but the kingdom? And Saul eyed David from that day and forward" (I Samuel 18:5–9).

Mature leadership would have known the danger of making such a comparison in song: "For we dare not make ourselves of the number, or compare ourselves with some that commend themselves: but they measuring themselves by themselves, and comparing themselves among themselves, are not wise" (II Corinthians 10:12). Whether evaluation of words or musical sound is being issued, those who are evaluating it must be mature. Both music and words have great potential for divisiveness and damage to God's kingdom, as is the case with all forms of communication. Both the message of the words and the message of the music itself need to be consistent with God's nature. In both cases, to avoid confusion and division, a Biblical standard is needed. In an electronic age in which our culture has become so saturated with music, it is vital that we examine and test our music.

Chapter 8

History of Music in America

ONE PRIMARY REASON FOR the wholesale acceptance of unclean music is a lack of maturity. My generation and I are responsible; in our youth group, we pursued fun and games more seriously than we pursued Christ through Bible study, Scripture memory, and evangelism of the lost. As a result, we failed to gain the maturity necessary to discern the spirit of the music that we accepted into our lives. The motivation for writing this book comes from a spirit of repentance and a new desire to fight the good fight of faith.

Many factors have contributed to the development of Contemporary Christian Music in the United States. Although there are more factors than this study examines (neo-orthodoxy is another factor that is discussed in Chapter 9), one of the main influences has been African tribal music. This chapter considers twelve stages of the development of Contemporary Christian Music in the United States.

Not all African music is unclean music, but this study will show how evil music in heathen African tribal worship has directly influenced the music we hear all around us today.

1. THE GARDEN OF EDEN

An understanding of what occurred in the original culture of the Garden of Eden provides a foundation for understanding what is going on in all other cultures today.

When Adam and Eve sinned, their guilt made them self-conscious and aware that they were separated from God. In a vain attempt to make themselves acceptable to God again, they tried to cover their bodies: "And the eyes of them both were opened, and they knew that they were naked; and they sewed fig leaves together, and made themselves aprons" (Genesis 3:7).

Being made in God's image, they had a God-consciousness, but when they looked at themselves they realized that something had been lost: they were not what they had been before; something was wrong; they experienced a new sense of shame and guilt. Where once there had been a unity between their physical nature and their spiritual nature, now there was a separation. In their spiritual nature they were consciously aware of God, but in their physical nature they were aware of sin and death: "But of the tree of the knowledge of good and evil, thou shalt not eat of it: for in the day that thou eatest thereof thou shalt surely die" (Genesis 2:17). "Wherefore, as by one man [Adam] sin entered into the world, and death by sin; and so death passed upon all men, for that all have sinned" (Romans 5:12).

Adam and Eve desperately wanted to cover up the results of their sin and clear their consciences, so in their own physical effort they made themselves aprons. They tried to eliminate the problem, to fill the vacuum and separation they felt and to restore the unity of their physical nature and their spiritual nature.

However, their efforts were fruitless. And in fact, the closer God drew near to them in the garden, the sharper they felt the sting of their consciences and the greater they sensed the failure of the aprons to remedy the dilemma: "And they heard the voice of the Lᴏʀᴅ God walking in the garden in the cool of the day: and Adam and his wife hid themselves from the presence of the Lᴏʀᴅ God amongst the trees of the garden" (Genesis 3:8). When they realized that their aprons could not do what was needed to restore their relationship with the Lord, they fled and hid themselves.

All societies and cultures try in one way or another to deal with the dilemma of this battle between the flesh and the spirit, the conflict between what we do in the body and what we know in our hearts we should do: "I find then a law, that, when I would do good, evil is present with me. For I delight in the law of God after the inward man: But I see another law in my members, warring against the law of my mind, and bringing me into captivity to the law of sin which is in my members. O wretched man that I am! who shall deliver me from the body of this death?" (Romans 7:21–24). The conflict in the Apostle Paul's soul is between what he knows in his mind is the right thing to do and what he often finds himself choosing to do, which in God's eyes is not the right thing to do.

> Where once there had been a unity between their physical nature and their spiritual nature, now there was a separation.

There is only one solution to this dilemma that each of us faces, and that is God's eternal plan of redemption. The action that God took on behalf of Adam and Eve after they sinned illustrates the initiative that God has taken on behalf of all mankind: "Unto Adam also and to his wife did the Lord God make coats of skins, and clothed them" (Genesis 3:21). In order for Adam and Eve's guilt to be cleared and their bodies—the very temple of God—restored, they had to put off what they had made themselves and accept the covering that God offered: coats of skins, which required the shedding of blood.

Restoration of harmony between the physical and spiritual can be achieved only as we confess our inadequacy and receive the Lord's sufficiency, which was offered through a sacrificial substitute, the Lord Jesus Christ. "And almost all things are by the law purged with blood; and without shedding of blood is no remission" (Hebrews 9:22).

The only hope of restoring harmony between the physical and the spiritual is a paradox, a mystery: "And he said to them all, If any man will come after me, let him deny himself, and take up his cross daily, and follow me. For whosoever will save his life shall lose it: but whosoever will lose his life for my sake, the same shall save it" (Luke 9:23–24). The paradox is that we must lose our life to save it. And we must lose it for the Lord's sake, that is, the sake of His Substitute. Those who save their lives, who seek happiness and restoration of the physical with the spiritual through some means or experience of self-expression, shall lose it.

It is futile to rely on natural efforts to change us, because our human nature is fallen and sinful. If we are to be changed, we must be transformed, born again, by God's supernatural power. The old self and its fleshly desires must die. Man naturally tries to save himself through some expression of himself, but only God can save man—as each person denies himself: "Knowing this, that our old man is crucified with him, that the body of sin might be destroyed, that henceforth we should not serve sin. For he that is dead is freed from sin. Now if we be dead with Christ, we believe that we shall also live with him" (Romans 6:6–8).

It would be helpful at this point to make a distinction between what we mean by "self-denial" and "denying oneself." Self-denial is simply an effort of the sinful self to improve itself by denying itself certain things. Self-denial may bring about varying degrees of success, but the sinful self does not die; it remains in control and reserves to itself the right to make the final decisions. However, to deny oneself as Jesus required in Luke Chapter 9 is to repent, to turn completely away from the sinful self in order to receive the life provided for us through God's Sacrificial Substitute.

> The paradox is that we must lose our life to save it.

One who denies himself is broken and humble. He has surrendered to Christ the right to make the final decisions for his life. Christ died and rose again. The only way any man will live with Christ is if he dies with Him: "Know ye not, that so many of us as were baptized into Jesus Christ were baptized into his death? Therefore we are buried with him by baptism into death: that like as Christ was raised up from the dead by the glory of the Father, even so we also should walk in newness of life" (Romans 6:3).

The only solution is death to, and separation from, the "body of sin" so that the new life of Christ may be lived through us: "That ye put off concerning the former conversation the old man, which is corrupt according to the deceitful lusts; and be renewed in the spirit of your mind; and that ye put on the new man, which after God is created in righteousness and true holiness" (Ephesians 4:22–24).

> The old prideful man, our flesh, does not like the thought of dying to self.

Not every culture deals with the dilemma of the separation between the physical and spiritual in this Biblical way. The old prideful man, our flesh, does not like the thought of dying to self, so Satan offers deceitful imitations. Let's look at one perverse way in which the heathen African tribal culture dealt with this separation.

2. AFRICAN TRIBAL WORSHIP

How did the African culture deal with this dilemma of the separation between the spiritual and the physical? In African tribal worship no separation between the *body of sin* and the *spirit* is sought. This worship is seen as a bodily celebration in which the goal is to experience with the body the intersection of the physical and spiritual worlds. [1]

The desire for this intersection is valid; it is what every culture attempts to achieve in one way or another. However, the means this culture used in its attempt to achieve this unity was not through denying oneself but rather through self-expression.

In this sense, their attempt was just what Adam and Eve initially tried to do in the garden.

Everything that happens during heathen African tribal worship to achieve this intersection takes place within the body. The symbol of this intersection is a cross in the form of a plus sign. It symbolizes the crossroad between the spiritual and the physical.[2] However, this cross is void of a sacrificial substitute and without any concept of repentance. "Christ hath redeemed us from the curse of the law, being made a curse for us: for it is written, Cursed is every one that hangeth on a tree: That the blessing of Abraham might come on the Gentiles through Jesus Christ; that we might receive the promise of the Spirit through faith" (Galatians 3:13–14).

> The means by which they attempt to achieve this intersection is primarily through the use of a drum.

The means by which they attempt to achieve this intersection is primarily through the use of a drum. The drum is regarded as sacred. It is worshipped, it is washed, it is fed, and it is rested. It is referred to as "the ear of god," and beating it is considered to be talking to it. The singers and dancers worship it and bow to it before they participate in the ceremony.[3]

The function of rhythm in this worship is to provide a structural beat as a catalyst of occult power. Other drums introduce multiple layers of rhythms, called polyrhythms, which induce a meditative state in which the worshippers' bodies literally become the crossroads of the physical and spiritual and are entered by one of their gods or goddesses.[4]

In Abomey, Benin, Africa, the deities that speak through humans are called *vodun*, meaning "mysteries." Each *vodun* prefers its own rhythm. The drummer makes them move as a unit, with groups swaying together in rhythm. The bodily movements of the participants help them to maintain contact with the main beat. Their worship is a powerful force that everyone feels. Everyone participates; there are no bystanders. [5]

The state of meditation that is induced by the rhythm is not a state of repentance and crucifixion of the "body of sin" but rather a state of self-expression and cutting loose of restraint in a search for fulfillment.

The rhythm of the drums communicates a message that directly opposes the gospel of Christ; it communicates a false gospel message. It preaches a lack of restraint that literally becomes for them a spiritual experience. However, it is a counterfeit experience with evil spirits.

Satan offers many substitutes for denying oneself and the filling of the Holy Spirit, and in the process he diverts worship to himself. He even tried to get Jesus Christ to worship him: "And saith unto him, All these things will I give thee, if thou wilt fall down and worship me" (Matthew 4:9). One of the greatest symbols of African heathen worship is the serpent, Satan: "And the great dragon was cast out, that old serpent, called the Devil, and Satan, which deceiveth the whole world: he was cast out into the earth, and his angels were cast out with him" (Revelation 12:9). Believers are warned to "be sober, be vigilant; because your adversary the devil, as a roaring lion, walketh about, seeking whom he may devour" (I Peter 5:8).

It should be noted at this point that such use of the drum is not unique to heathen African tribal worship. Ways that the beat of the drum was used in heathen New Guinea tribal ceremonies to impress the senses will be described in Chapter 10. For them, the medium of the music was the message of no restraint, a means of self-expression through which they told their gruesome stories of treachery.

3. SLAVERY IN THE WEST INDIES

Slavery existed among African tribes before the Europeans arrived. Strong tribes enslaved weak tribes and sold them as slaves to other tribes. When the Europeans arrived, African tribes were enslaved and sold to European merchants who took them to the West Indies (Haiti and Cuba).

The slaves continued practicing their tribal ceremonies in the West Indies and passed instruction to the next generation about how to possess the gods bodily. In voodoo, the worship of African slaves was forced to change as a result of their new circumstances, that of being transported from Africa to a new location. As slaves from different tribes were forced to be together, tribal elements were combined and things that were done in the same way were retained, while differences were discarded.[6]

> The slaves continued practicing their tribal ceremonies in the West Indies and passed instruction to the next generation . . .

Heathen tribal worship was easily blended with the Catholic influences in the West Indies. The worship of icons and saints introduced the idea of picturing their gods, and consequently images of serpents with St. Patrick were generated. It is interesting to note that while Catholicism and Voodoo blend well, Protestantism and Voodoo are always at odds. Many Africans professed Catholicism freely, but if they made their gods angry, they became Protestants to protect themselves and free them from the wrath of their gods. A Haitian saying says, "If you want the *loa* [a voodoo god] to leave you alone—become a Protestant." It was observed that some slaves desired to become Protestants, not out of faith, but because they saw Protestantism as a magic circle of refuge from the gods who were displeased with them and sought to do them harm.[7]

Like opportunistic germs, heathen influences are ever on the move looking for opportunities to infiltrate, mix with pure religion, and kill. The significance of these historical observations is that they demonstrate the need for continual resistance against the attempts of the unclean to mix with the clean: "And what agreement hath the temple of God with idols? for ye are the temple of the living God; as God hath said, I will dwell in them, and walk in them; and I will be their God, and they shall be my people. Wherefore come out from among them, and be ye separate, saith the Lord, and touch not the unclean thing; and I will receive you, And will be a Father unto you, and ye shall be my sons and daughters, saith the Lord Almighty" (II Corinthians 6:16-18).

4. SLAVERY IN NORTH AMERICA

Many African slaves were transported to North America through the appalling slave trade. Though their ceremonies and drums were legally forbidden in colonial America, the slaves still did what they could to pass on their worship traditions. They developed forms of intricate foot tapping and vocalization of nonsense syllables in rhythmic patterns.[8] Only one city in the South allowed these ceremonies: New Orleans, a city with many free blacks (14% of its population in 1788 and practically 20% of its population in 1805).[9] The ceremonies were permitted as a gathering for "entertainments." Prior to the Louisiana Purchase, New Orleans was a Spanish and French city, the only major city in the United States that was neither Anglo-Saxon nor Protestant.[10]

The Haitian Slave Revolution of 1791 brought a huge surge of immigrants who began making drums. Often these drums were played in secret defiance of their slave owners.[11]

In 1817 slaves were forbidden to congregate except in specific places on Sundays. One such place in New Orleans was Congo Square, where the ceremonies took on a Western form of "presentation" with an audience of whites watching. The overt religious elements were concealed within the music to avoid offending observers.[12] Recall the description of Satan stated in Revelation 12:9: ". . . the Devil, and Satan, which deceiveth the whole world . . . ." To introduce a false gospel to the American culture, entertainment became Satan's new disguise.

> To introduce a false gospel to the American culture, entertainment became Satan's new disguise.

Dance styles such as Samba, Conga, and Mamba were named for voodoo gods. For example, *Samba* is derived from the West African Bantu word *semba*, meaning "invoke the spirit of the ancestors."[13] It was not until about 1917 that Brazilian authorities permitted participants at the Rio Carnival to play samba music.[14]

The pagan rhythms had an influence on the religious camp meetings of the 1800s, although the slaves commonly remained seated outside the meeting places. Rhythmic music did not originate in these camp meetings, but rather it was brought into them with a contradictory message. The problem of the contradictory messages was noted at that time: "While the white masters were singing hymns in careful measures, their slaves would be shouting the same song and beating out stirring counter rhythms on tambourines, gourds, and logs. When the excitement spread, infusing the slave rhythms into the Protestant church liturgy, the country witnessed the frenzy of hysterical revival meetings and shouting Sunday meetings."[15] Where do you distinguish the difference between the spiritual and more secular enthusiasm? The following inconsistency is voiced by an unbeliever: "A religion of denial [Christianity] worshipped with a religious practice that is anything but denial [pagan rhythms] . . ." will result in ". . . the church sending out two contradictory signals at the same time, one to the body and one to the mind. A doctrine that denied the body, preached by a practice that excited the body, would eventually drive the body

> Rhythmic music did not originate in these camp meetings, but rather it was brought into them with a contradictory message.

into fulfilling itself elsewhere."[16] What occurs is a doctrine in word that denies the body (the lower sinful nature) preached by a practice in music that excites the body (self-expression without self-restraint).

Consider the widespread anecdote describing a frog being slowly boiled alive. As we progress through the various stages of the history of music in the United States, we can see how the frog, our spiritual Christian heritage, is sitting in a pot of water, the secular influence of a false gospel, and is slowly boiled alive as the fiery influence of worldliness progressively increases over decades of time.

5. THE BLUES (AROUND 1800)

The term *blues* is a shortened version of the term *blue devils*, which is a reference to demons popularly thought to cause depression and sadness. Blues music originated primarily within the African-American communities in the Deep South of the United States.[17]

Blues music is melancholy music that was initially created by slaves who had been deprived of drums and rituals. Its development included polyrhythms with a syncopated swing and an implicit beat. It includes a visible bodily response that is not always heard but always felt—felt, due to the rhythm. The lyrical emphasis is on the fleshly pleasures of this world. The musical techniques employed to communicate the lyrical sensuality include moaning vocals and pitch-bending instrumentals. The blues notes are slightly under pitch on certain tones.[18]

"Fundamentally, blues was by tradition a secular music belonging to the theaters, clubs, drinking dens, and brothels;

and concerns of the flesh—sexuality, the next meal, hitting the road in search of work—provided its main subject matter."[19]

Storyville was the "red light district" of New Orleans. The bars and brothels of this part of town, which became known for the perversion that was welcomed there, became the home of the blues music. The message communicated by the blues rhythm continues to proclaim the false gospel of self-expression and excitement of the body of sin. There is no call for denial of self or repentance from sin—in fact, just the opposite is encouraged.

While the heathen African tradition of possession by a spirit god was still present, through the development of blues music an explicit emphasis on possession by a spirit of sensuality was introduced.

6. EARLY JAZZ (1890)

The United States was influenced spiritually by the ministries of Charles Finney (1792–1875), D. L. Moody (1837–1899), Robert Sheffey (1820–1902), and Fanny Crosby (1820–1915). Fanny Crosby is the greatest hymn writer that ever lived, writing over 9,000 songs. Before Fanny Crosby was saved, at 45 years old, she wrote many secular songs. After her salvation Fanny Crosby expressed concern about the mixing of Christian and worldly music: "Sometimes I need to reject the music proposed for my songs because the musicians misunderstand that the Fanny Crosby who once wrote for the people in

> "The church must never sing its songs to the melodies of the world."

the saloons has merely changed the lyrics. Oh my no. The church must never sing its songs to the melodies of the world."[20]

The perverse lyrics of the blues had their parallel elements in the musical tones of jazz. During the same period of history, Buddy Bolden (1877–1930) became the first jazz musician to play African blues on European instruments. Early jazz included a subtle reappearance of voodoo. Images such as the "long snake" appeared lyrically in many of the early blues and jazz songs. Veiled descriptions of voodoo practices also included the trance-like state of the performers.[21] Slang African terminology such as *mojo* ("soul; an object invested with spirit power and the capacity to heal or influence"), *boogy* ("devilishly good"), *juke* ("bad"), and *jazz* ("the act of immorality"). Other terms of African origin are *funky*, *hippie*, *rap*, and *dig*.[22]

> Would the growing acceptance of this music become popular enough to overturn laws that were in harmony with the moral values of our Puritan forefathers?

At this point Jazz was heard only in the bad part of town. However, with the new acceptance of this style of music that was now played on European instruments, the frog was in the water, and the temperature was being turned up. Would the growing acceptance of this music become popular enough to overturn laws that were in harmony with the moral values of our Puritan forefathers? Even in its mildest form, the musical message of the new rhythm was a direct rejection of the need for separation from the body of sin. "Knowing this, that our old man is crucified with him, that the body of sin might be destroyed, that henceforth we should not serve sin" (Romans 6:6). (See also Romans 7:22–25.)

7. THE JAZZ ERA (EARLY 1900S)

If we fail to learn from history, we are doomed to repeat it. The book of Judges reveals a cycle of events that is difficult for a culture to escape unless its people are eternally vigilant. Following times of peace and prosperity, the Israelites began doing what was right in their own eyes and fell into apostasy. God would then send an oppressor to call Israel to repentance. Following repentance, God would send a deliverer who brought peace and prosperity again.

The turn of the century brought such prosperity to the United States. These were the times of Thomas Edison (1847–1931), Alexander Graham Bell (1847–1922), and Albert Einstein (1879–1955). There were inventions in flight and in automobiles. Through radio, sound began going across the ocean, and the *Titanic* set out on its maiden voyage. However, with these rapid advances in technology, people developed a feeling that they could not keep up with all the changes. People in general were more nervous and afraid because of low pay and harsh work. Child labor was an issue.

God provided spiritual influences to keep the United States vigilant and anchored to its Christian heritage through the ministries of men like Billy Sunday (1862–1935) and Dawson Trotman, founder of the Navigators (1906–1956); followed by Billy Graham (1918–present) and Bill Bright, founder of Campus Crusade for Christ (1921–2003). However, in general, Americans did not recognize the spiritual dangers that came with the changing times but instead trusted in their own understanding and welcomed untested music that expressed their feelings.

Orderly music communicates the message that the body submits to the spirit, but many people became dissatisfied with this type of music. It did not reflect what they were experiencing, so they sought a different kind of music that agreed with their experience.

As a compromise, composers like Sott Joplin introduced ragtime music. This music was less traditional and still had some order, but it was not the perverse blues. It had a "ragged" rhythm and was highly syncopated. It communicated a frantic air of the new while retaining the poise of the respectable. Dances were wilder but still with decorum.

The world had gone mad with the First World War (1914–1918). The confusion in the world was reflected by the Original Dixieland Jazz Band that first appeared in New Orleans in 1917. This style of music was polyphonic, that is, all instruments were played simultaneously but presented unique variations of the melody. All the different parts were improvised over a dominant beat. Decorum in dance styles like the Charleston were no longer possible.

> Orderly music communicates the message that the body submits to the spirit . . .

Because of problems of disorderly conduct that occurred when many sailors visited Storyville, the Secretary of the Navy shut down this district—an excellent decision. However, human hearts were left unchanged, and therefore jazz spread up the Mississippi River, appearing in Memphis, St. Louis, Chicago, etc.

This was the time of Al Capone (1899–1947) and prohibition. Joseph King Oliver, the mentor and teacher of Louis Armstrong, gained fame during this era. Other successful jazz musicians included Sidney Bechet and "Jelly Roll" Morton. Mr. Morton, whose godmother was a voodoo priestess, wrote the first jazz composition ever published. Louis Armstrong, the "King of Swing," introduced new jazz features such as nonsense rhythmic syllables, called scatt singing.

The jazz era included the roaring twenties. Tap dancing became popular. Minstrel shows, in which whites dressed up like blacks, became a part of the popular culture. It is ironic that while black entertainment styles were admired and imitated, black people remained objects of ridicule, as evidenced by the actions of the Ku Klux Klan.

> ... the downfall of one thousand girls could be traced directly to the pernicious influence of jazz music.

Al Jolson popularized a large number of songs characterized by his "shamelessly sentimental, melodramatic approach."[23] His performing style was brash and extroverted. Numerous well-known singers were influenced by his music, including Bob Dylan, who once referred to Al Jolson as "somebody whose life I can feel."[24]

All men are seeking the restoration of harmony between the physical and spiritual in their search for lasting happiness. It is not achieved through subjective stimulation of the feelings but rather through the objective preaching of the gospel: "For after that in the wisdom of God the world by wisdom knew not God, it pleased God by the foolishness of preaching to save them that believe" (I Corinthians 1:21). The message of unrestrained living preached by jazz music is not the message of complete surrender to the lordship of Christ.

The following transcript is from a PBS radio broadcast: "'Moral disaster is coming to hundreds of young American girls,' reported the *New York American*, 'through the pathological, nerve irritating, sex-exciting music of jazz orchestras.' In just two years in Chicago alone, the Illinois Vigilance Association reported in 1923, the downfall of one thousand girls could be traced directly to the pernicious influence of jazz music. In Cincinnati, the Salvation Army obtained a court injunction to stop construction of a theater next to a home for expectant mothers on the grounds that 'the enforced proximity of a theater and jazz palace' would implant dangerous 'jazz emotions' in helpless infants. A social worker reported on the 'unwholesome excitement' she now encountered even at small-town dances in the Midwest. 'Boy-and-girl couples leave the hall in a state of dangerous disturbance. Any worker who has gone into the night to gather the facts of activities outside the dance hall is appalled . . . by the blatant disregard of even the elementary rules of civilization . . . . We must expect a few casualties in social discourse, but the modern dance is producing little short of holocaust.'"[25]

> Because America did not remain vigilant in times of social prosperity, she fell into moral depravity.

Because America did not remain vigilant in times of social prosperity, she fell into moral depravity. The frog is in the water and the temperature is on high.

8. BIG BAND JAZZ (1930S)

During this era, familiarity took over. Personal preference, rather than the divine revelation of Biblical truth, became the basis of moral decisions. Prohibition was lifted and jazz followed alcohol on the road to social acceptance. Big-band jazz took over the ballrooms of the Roosevelt Era during the war years.

"Duke" Ellington (1899–1974) was one of the most influential figures in jazz. When asked what inspired him to write, Ellington replied: "My men and my race are the inspiration of my work. I try to catch the character and mood and feeling of my people."[26] While his intentions were noble, the message in Ellington's music does not communicate the mood and spirit of Christ, Who alone is the true source of character for any people. Rather, the message in Ellington's music communicates the false spirit of his ancestors' religion, a message of a lack of restraint that is in direct opposition to the gospel of Christ. One of Ellington's most popular pieces, titled "Ko-Ko," was inspired by African drumbeats.

9. RHYTHM AND BLUES (1940S—THE POST-WAR YEARS)

The economic restraints in post-war years forced swing bands to reduce their size. Electrically amplified instruments came into use. Rhythm and Blues (R&B) featured a solo singer accompanied by a small jazz band.

Performers included Bessie Smith, Johnny Otis, Nat King Cole, B.B. King, Julia Lee, and many others. R&B band instruments included the electric guitar, drums, bass, harmonica, and occasionally a saxophone and/or piano.

R&B is another form of jazz. R&B rhythms also communicate the message of self-expression. Although primarily the music of black musicians, it soon began to be discovered and imitated by white musicians. Elvis Presley and Jerry Lee Louis would sneak out of the house at night to listen to this new type of music. [27]

10. EARLY ROCK 'N' ROLL (1950S)

Early Rock 'n' Roll (R&R) combined elements of R&B with country/western. Bill Haley and the Comets wrote "Shake, Rattle, and Roll," and "Rock Around the Clock." Other performers of early R&R included Little Richard, Fats Domino, and Chuck Berry, and their music was soon heard on public radio.

The music of Elvis Presley (1935–1977) created a great demand for R&R; every part of Elvis's body was in tune with his music. Nobody had ever seen a "white boy" with moves like Elvis had. In June 1956, Elvis made the following statement about R&R to a reporter in Charlotte, North Carolina: "The colored folks been singing it and playing it just like I'm doin' now, man, for more years than I know. They played it like that in their shanties and in their juke joints and nobody paid it no mind 'til I goosed it up. I got it from them. Down in Tupelo, Mississippi, I used to hear old Arthur Crudup bang his box the way I do now and I said if I ever got to a place I could feel all old Arthur felt, I'd be a music man like nobody ever saw." [28]

To his credit he also said: "I am not the King. Jesus Christ is the King. I'm just an entertainer." [29] However, Elvis confessed: "I don't know anything about music. In my line you don't have to." [30] Elvis may have sung about crying in the chapel, but the cry in the message of the music he performed did not reflect the holy nature of the God of the Bible. His concerts drew crowds to himself, his entertainment style, and a lifestyle of self-expression; they did not draw crowds to the cross of Christ.

The true source of life and happiness is found in the presence of God: ". . . In thy presence is fullness of joy; at thy right hand there are pleasures for evermore" (Psalm 16:11). The path to true fulfillment is found in a personal relationship with Jesus Christ, not in the temporary pleasures of entertainment: "Jesus saith unto him, I am the way, the truth, and the life: no man cometh unto the Father, but by me" (John 14:6). When a person looks to something in his life to meet a need that only God can meet, then that thing becomes an idol. Therefore, if a person looks to entertainment to meet the need for joy and fulfillment, then entertainment becomes a substitute for God; it becomes an idol.

> When a person looks to something in his life to meet a need that only God can meet, then that thing becomes an idol.

The *New York Daily News* reported, "Elvis took the subversive words and rhythms from all the places middle class Americans preferred not to be bothered with: coal towns, farms, dark inner cities, dirty roadside cafes, and he deposited them on the bright clean living room carpet."[31] This style of music proclaims the lie that the body can be united with the spirit (fulfillment can be felt) without the need for a sacrificial substitute and without the need for repentance and holy, Christ-like living. The false message communicated to youth via worldly music is to not restrain yourself but rather to let yourself go, to feel the rhythm, and to let the spirit of the music enter into you. It is a false spirit, a perverse alternative to the filling of the Holy Spirit.

Although R&R music became accepted as a respectable form of entertainment, it preserved the qualities of African voodoo by imitating the same sounds and bodily motions demonstrated by the Africans who were possessed or ridden by the gods. Modern R&R preserves these pagan qualities so strongly that it unconsciously generates the same behavior and ". . . uses a derivative of voodoo's technique of possession as a source for energy for both the performer and the audience."[32]

The voodoo concept of possession became the standard of American performances in R&R, whose performers ". . . let themselves be possessed not by any god that they could name but by the spirit they felt in the music. Their behavior in this possession was something Western society had never before tolerated. And the way a possessed devotee in a Voodoo ceremony often will transmit his state of possession to someone else is by merely touching the hand; Western performers transmit their possession through their voice and their dance to their audience, even through their records."[33]

An article about the history of recording reported that as the music of this time period became popular, the youth market was created. Youth began to emerge as a group themselves, with their own ideas and their own philosophies.[34] The article explained how this was a fundamental, structural change in American society that would eventually result in far-reaching social changes. The thread that ran through all the notable youth movements of the 1960s (anti-war, civil rights, feminism, ecology, higher-consciousness, etc.) and continues in their derivatives now was a fundamental challenge to the recognition of the need to separate the spirit from the body of sin. This challenge, which defined the mood of the 1960s generation, was implied in their music. Parents seemed hesitant to guard their family from these influences because of false fears of alienating their children and damaging their children's self-image and self-expression.

> "We take kids away from their parents and their environment to where the only reality is the rhythm and the beat."

Here is a sad statement in regard to the youth market by Donnie Brewer of Grand Funk: "We take kids away from their parents and their environment to where the only reality is the rhythm and the beat."[35]

The water is rapidly boiling around the apparently hapless frog.

11. ROCK MUSIC (1960S)

The Beatles' music was less abrasive, so it became known as just "rock." It resulted in the widening of the range of popular music. This era in music included Woodstock and the hippie movement.

One technique that is used to widen the range of a particular style of music is called crossover music. Crossover music waters down music's distinctive qualities to accommodate mass tastes.

For example, in the early years of R&R, many songs originally recorded by African-American musicians were re-recorded by white artists in a more toned-down style, often with changed lyrics that lacked the hard edge of the original versions. These recordings were popular with a much broader audience.

Once a new style becomes acceptable, the hard edge is re-introduced. Thus, following the popularity of the Beatles' music, the Rolling Stones' music featured an emphasis on the occult, drugs, and promiscuity. In 1994 they took their Voodoo Lounge Tour to the entire world.

12. AND ON TO THE PRESENT

Within the human soul, there is an insatiable appetite for more, which a false spirit cannot fulfill, as evidenced by heavy metal, punk rock, acid rock, etc. Profanity and pop music go hand in hand these days. On her blog, *The Record*, NPR music critic Ann Powers declared, "21st century pop music is very dirty." She observed that "2011 saw so much boundary-breaking in pop that the lines seem forever pulled down."[36] The message of self-expression is very much alive in music performed today.

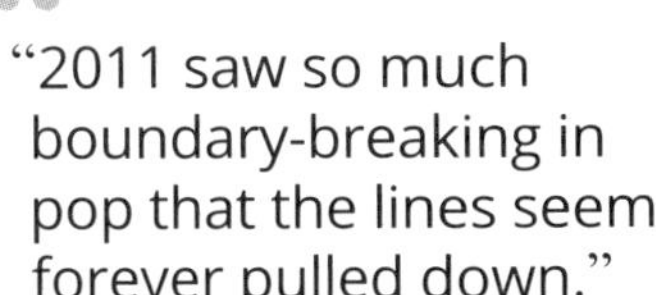

The more the Bible and its principles are removed from United States culture, the greater will be the damage to spiritual maturity, the greater will be the spiritual darkness, and the greater will be the influence of unclean spirits.

Is there anything left of the frog?

Some Conclusions

- African roots are not the only roots of rock music; however, there is no question that there is a strong African connection to the rock rhythm of our day.

- There is clear historical proof that demonic activity has been observed in connection with rituals where drums and rhythmic beats have been the catalyst

- History shows that musical forms reproduce themselves in human conduct. Unclean worldly music communicates the message that there need not be any separation between the body of sin and the spirit. Why, then, are we allowing such music in our churches?

  "Love not the world, neither the things that are in the world. If any man love the world, the love of the Father is not in him. For all that is in the world, the lust of the flesh, and the lust of the eyes, and the pride of life, is not of the Father, but is of the world" (I John 2:15–16)

  "Ye adulterers and adulteresses, know ye not that the friendship of the world is enmity with God? whosoever therefore will be a friend of the world is the enemy of God" (James 4:4).

- Satan can and will use anything in his power to turn mankind away from the worship of a holy God so that he might ultimately divert worship to himself.

My trust and prayer is that this study will motivate you to study the subject more seriously on your own, that it will result in deeper Biblical convictions, and that it will equip you to join in the battle for truth.

CHAPTER 9

Contemporary Trends of Music in the United States

WHICH IS MORE IMPORTANT: what we believe or the fact that we believe? Your answer to this question reveals how much you have been influenced by the vain philosophy of neo-orthodoxy.

1. THE EMPTY DECEIT OF VAIN PHILOSOPHIES

"Beware lest any man spoil you through philosophy and vain deceit, after the tradition of men, after the rudiments of the world, and not after Christ" (Colossians 2:8). *Philosophy* means "a love of wisdom." Unfortunately, much of the education in the United States focuses on a love of knowledge rather than a love of the wisdom that is needed to maintain moral purity, unite a marriage, or raise godly children. It is vain because it is empty or void of Christ. It is based on the popular rudiments of the world and leaves Christ out. The result is a state where one professes himself wise but is foolish in his behavior: "Because that, when they knew God, they glorified him not as God, neither were thankful; but became vain in their imaginations, and their foolish heart was darkened. Professing themselves to be wise, they became fools" (Romans 1:21–22).

Like heathen African religious worship, neo-orthodoxy, which originated in Europe, is an attempt to get back to the euphoric experience of the Garden of Eden apart from divine revelation. Neo-orthodoxy is a pseudo-religious attempt to find ways to affirm the authority and truth of Scripture without viewing it as historically accurate or literally true in all cases.

It holds that because the Bible contains mistakes, it contains only partial truth about God and is not the inerrant Word of God. Thus, it separates "religious truth" from the "historical truth" of the Scriptures. We are told to just believe the Bible without objective analysis and verification, only as a subjective "leap of faith."

> Man cannot do anything to save himself, but he can objectively search the Scriptures.

As affirmed by the Protestant reformers of the sixteenth century, the Scriptures say that man cannot do anything to save himself, but he can objectively search the Scriptures. (See Acts 17:11 and II Timothy 2:15.) These Scriptures reveal not only truth about God but also truth about history and the nature of the universe. (See Romans 1:18–21, Colossians 2:3, and Ephesians 1:9–11.)

As divine revelation is rejected, faith becomes a leap into a subjective experience without objective verification. "Consequently, what really forms the 'Christ-like' act today is simply what the consensus of the church or the consensus of society makes up its mind is desirable at that particular moment."[1] What is practiced is merely a set of relative morals.

Historical Biblical thinking involves opposites: good—bad, united—divided, true—false, heaven—hell. Carl Barth led the teaching of neo-orthodoxy by introducing the concept that there was no absolute right or wrong. Instead, good was not always good, bad was not always bad, and truth was logically or emotionally determined to lie somewhere between these two.

This philosophy begins with a "thesis" (statement) and an "antithesis" (opposing statement) and arrives at truth through a process called "synthesis," which is relativism. Through synthesis this philosophy would say that the Bible is "inspired," but what is meant by inspired is no different than Shakespeare being inspired. Through synthesis this philosophy would say that Jesus is the "son of god," but what is meant by a son of god is no different than everyone being a son of god.

The term *neo-orthodox* itself is misleading. It is not new and it is not orthodox. Because neo-orthodoxy does not define religious truth objectively according to Scripture, words with strong connotations from the memory of our Christian heritage are used to give an illusion of communication; terminology like *inspiration*, *son of god*, *resurrection*, *crucifixion*, and *Jesus* are used but never defined.

Without divine revelation, there is no certainty of spiritual reality. Being made in the image of God and having a God consciousness, man cannot live merely as a machine, as though he is nothing. So, out of despair, he is forced to seek some type of leap of faith, some type of mystical experience, some type of search for lasting happiness.

He places in his God-shaped vacuum all sorts of desperate things or experiences. Warren Wiersbe, in his book *The Integrity*

Crisis, observes that there is a brand of Christianity that is frightening to behold; they are ". . . living on substitutes and don't know it." The Word of God addresses this circumstance in the book of Galatians: "I marvel that ye are so soon removed from him that called you into the grace of Christ unto another gospel: Which is not another; but there be some that trouble you, and would pervert the gospel of Christ. But though we, or an angel from heaven, preach any other gospel unto you than that which we have preached unto you, let him be accursed. As we said before, so say I now again, If any man preach any other gospel unto you than that ye have received, let him be accursed" (Galatians 1:6–9).

> Jesus warned of the serious danger of being caught up in religious experiences that do not reflect what He is truly like.

Whatever the experience, if it is separated from the gospel and from Christlike character, it takes on a form of self-expression rather than self-restraint. This self-expression may be manifested in a variety of ways, including drugs, pornography, sodomy, paintings, music, novels, nature, drama, hobbies, sports, good works, or religion.

Jesus warned of the serious danger of being caught up in religious experiences that do not reflect what He is truly like: "Many will say to me in that day, Lord, Lord, have we not prophesied in thy name? and in thy name have cast out devils? and in thy name done many wonderful works? And then will I profess unto them, I never knew you: depart from me, ye that work iniquity" (Matthew 7:22–23).

Let's take a closer look at some of the vain efforts of neo-orthodoxy to find fulfillment:

- Aldous Huxley advocated the use of drugs in order to have a first-order experience. You take a drug in order to try to have a direct mystical experience.[2]

  This is similar to the motives for welcoming demon possession during heathen African tribal worship. It is a false experience that is generated in an effort to try to get back to the spiritual reality that was lost in the Garden of Eden. This first-order experience has no relation to the objective truth of God's Word, fails to set forth the need for repentance, does not acknowledge the need for a personal Savior, and does not declare the need for a new birth.

- The need for an undefined leap of faith has been expressed in poetry. Martin Heidegger, in his book *What Is Philosophy?,* ends with the admonition to "look to the poet." What he means is that the content of the poem is immaterial; one might have six poets all contradicting each other; what matters is that such a thing as poetry exists. Because poetry exists, one hopes in some desperate, undefined leap that there is more to life than mere existence.[3]

- The same is true in art. The confusion of abstract art reflects the uncertainty and confusion that result from the rejection of a God of order and His demand for a righteous way of life. Nevertheless, having been created in the image of God, one still hopes through the existence of art to find meaning in life. Again, because art exists, one hopes in some desperate, undefined way to resolve the paradox of man's goodness at times and man's sinfulness at other times. [4]

- The same is true in music. The confusion, high tension, and battering of the senses by worldly music that has no rules reflects the uncertainty that results from the rejection of a God of order and His demand for righteous living. Nevertheless, having been made in the image of God, one still hopes through the existence of music to find meaning in life.

- In one example of sensual writing, a woman puts herself into a man's hands to be beaten. The work explicitly states that because no God exists, the woman wants to be possessed by someone, and thus, in her alienation, is glad of the beatings and pain as a proof of possession by something, someone. [5] God created us with a proper desire to be loved and possessed by the Holy Spirit. However, this writing shows the extreme desperation to which men fall when God's truth and His ways are rejected. Apart from God, men are seduced by false substitutes.

Neo-orthodoxy is not a new idea. Its tenets have gradually crept into many well-founded institutions. For example, Christians originally founded Harvard as a missionary school. When, like a little leaven, neo-orthodox ideas were mingled with Christian teachings, the founders left Harvard and founded Yale in an effort to establish an institution that would support truth. We should follow their example and refuse to mix the philosophies contained in worldly music with the truths contained in God's Word.

It is significant to learn who Francis Schaeffer observed to be the teachers of neo-orthodoxy: "The interesting thing today is that . . . the real philosophic expressions have tended to pass over to those who do not occupy the chairs of philosophy—the novelist, the film producer, the jazz musician, the hippies, and even teenage gangs in their violence."[6] The jazz musician is teaching philosophic expressions not only through words but, more deceitfully, also through the style of the music itself.

> It is significant to learn who Francis Schaeffer observed to be the teachers of neo-orthodoxy . . .

"Let no man deceive you with vain words: for because of these things cometh the wrath of God upon the children of disobedience" (Ephesians 5:6). We must be alert not only to ensure that no man deceives us with vain words but also to ensure that no man deceives us with vain art or vain music.

2. THE PERPETRATION OF AN UNDEFINED JESUS

The "leap of faith" can take many forms—some religious, some secular, some dirty, some clean. The type of words does not matter, including such a well-loved word as *Jesus*:

The word is used as a content-less (undefined) banner, and our generation is invited to follow it. But there is no rational, Scriptural content by which to test it, and thus the word Jesus is being used to teach the very opposite things from those which Jesus taught. . . . It is now Jesus-like to sleep with a girl or a man, if she or he needs you. As long as you are trying to be human you are being

Jesus-like to sleep with the other person, at the cost, be it noted, of breaking the specific morality that Jesus taught.

We must fight this content-less banner, with its deep motivations, rooted into the memories of the race, which is being used for the purpose of sociological form and control. . . . If evangelical Christians begin to slip into a dichotomy, to separate an encounter with Jesus from the content of the Scriptures (including the discussable and the verifiable), we shall, without intending to, be throwing ourselves and the next generation into the mill-stream of the modern system. This system surrounds us as an almost monolithic consensus. [7]

"But I fear, lest by any means, as the serpent beguiled Eve through his subtlety, so your minds should be corrupted from the simplicity that is in Christ. For if he that cometh preacheth another Jesus, whom we have not preached, or if ye receive another spirit, which ye have not received, or another gospel, which ye have not accepted, ye might well bear with him" (II Corinthians 11:4). It is just as easy to fall into this error today as it was in the first century.

"The old philosophers always said that there was somebody there, but the new philosophers say that does not matter, because faith is the important thing. It is faith in faith, whether expressed in secular or religious terms. The leap is the thing and not the terms in which the leap is expressed. The verbalization, i.e. the symbol systems, can change; whether they use one word or another is incidental. Modern man is committed to finding his answer upstairs, by a leap, away from rationality and away from reason." [8]

The phrase *finding answers upstairs* is a way to express the attempt to get back to the Garden of Eden to find meaning and true happiness. The leap is merely a mystical hope of a divine experience. The leap is a false substitute for the true restoration of harmony between the physical and the spiritual through repentance and denial of self. "And he said to them all, If any man will come after me, let him deny himself, and take up his cross daily, and follow me. For whosoever will save his life shall lose it: but whosoever will lose his life for my sake, the same shall save it" (Luke 9:23–24).

> Faith is only as valid as the object of faith. Sincerity alone does not validate one's faith.

Faith is only as valid as the object of faith. Sincerity alone does not validate one's faith. "Now faith is the substance of things hoped for, the evidence of things not seen" (Hebrews 11:1). The remainder of Hebrews chapter 11 gives specific examples of the truths that many heroes of faith have believed. There is no recorded instance of any Biblical hero whose faith was merely faith in faith.

One tragic result of neo-orthodoxy is the false conclusion that all religions lead to heaven. If what one believes gets lost in some mystical faith in faith, then all religions could be said to be the same. Wouldn't this help set the stage for a one-world religious ruler? In contrast, "Jesus saith unto him, I am the way, the truth, and the life: no man cometh unto the Father, but by me" (John 14:6).

The world is presenting a counterfeit Jesus. In 1971 the stage production of *Jesus Christ Superstar* presented Jesus as a man who was as twisted and mixed up as Judas was. That same year the musical *Godspell* opened on Broadway and presented Jesus as a clown, making Him out to be a joke. Then in 1988 the film *The Last Temptation of Christ* presented Jesus as a sinner.

Note that *Jesus Christ Superstar* is called a "rock opera," and *Godspell* has been defined as "lite rock" that is "a fluffy piece intended for children, with 'cool' young adults who sing *pop* music."[9] Wrong doctrine regarding the nature of Christ's character is made to appear more acceptable by means of the popular (but unclean) music that accompanies it.

"Wherefore should the heathen say, Where is now their God? But our God is in the heavens: he hath done whatsoever he hath pleased. Their idols are silver and gold, the work of men's hands. They have mouths, but they speak not: eyes have they, but they see not: They have ears, but they hear not: noses have they, but they smell not: They have hands, but they handle not: feet have they, but they walk not: neither speak they through their throat. They that make them are like unto them; so is every one that trusteth in them. O Israel, trust thou in the LORD: he is their help and their shield. O house of Aaron, trust in the LORD: he is their help and their shield. Ye that fear the LORD, trust in the LORD: he is their help and their shield" (Psalm 115:2–11).

> The world is presenting a counterfeit Jesus.

The object of the Christian faith is not a content-less Christ without historical reality but rather is a living Lord Who "died for our sins according to the scriptures; and that he was buried, and that he rose again the third day according to the scriptures" (I Corinthians 15:3–4).

3. THE PERVADING DANGERS OF WORLDLY MUSIC

"The melodies in New Age music are often repetitive to create a hypnotic feeling, and sometimes recordings of nature sounds are used as an introduction to a track or throughout the piece. Pieces of up to thirty minutes are common. . . . New Age music is defined more by the effect or feeling it produces rather than the instruments used in its creation; it may be electronic, acoustic, or a mixture of both."[10]

Characteristics of New Age music include short, repeated motives; repeated patterns; lack of variety; and little or no melody. Ideas are sustained without change. There is little sense of form and no rules, which communicates the message that there is no right and no wrong, no beginning and no ending. New Age music is characterized by ambient sound, the feeling of being surrounded by sound. The music communicates the message without words.

Music that is defined merely by its abstract effects and feelings reflect the New Age "content-less banner" described earlier in this chapter.

> New Age music is defined more by the effect or feeling it produces.

This style of music perpetrates the false message that a mystical leap can fill man's God-shaped void. In contrast, we must bring every thought captive to Christ to avoid the risk of believing lies about Him and about life: "Casting down imaginations, and every high thing that exalteth itself against the knowledge of God, and bringing into captivity every thought to the obedience of Christ" (II Corinthians 10:5).

Dangers of New Age music that divert us from worshipping God in spirit and in truth include these:

Communicating Careless Emotional Messages Through the Musical Style

Beware of careless musical messages communicated in the music of the world. One careless emotional message in New Age-style music is that there is no absolute truth in life, only relativism. The tenets of relativism are that there is no absolute good or evil, no absolute right or wrong, and no acceptance of the Bible as the final authority in all matters of life and practice, but rather an imagined evolutionary process toward a higher state. [11]

The lack of structure, melody, and order in New Age music hinders the discipline required for the Word of Christ to dwell in us richly through Bible reading, Bible study, Bible memorization, and Scriptural meditation. "Let the word of Christ dwell in you richly in all wisdom; teaching and admonishing one another in psalms and hymns and spiritual songs, singing with grace in your hearts to the Lord" (Colossians 3:16).

Another careless musical message found in New Age style music is amusement. Musical style reflects a school of thought. In the book *Amusing Ourselves to Death*, Neil Postman observes: "Christianity is a demanding and serious religion. When it is delivered as easy and amusing it is a different kind of religion altogether." [12] In the essay *On popular music*,

Theodor W. Adorno states: "The frame of mind to which popular music originally appealed, on which it feeds, and which it perpetually reinforces, is simultaneously one of distraction and inattention. Listeners are distracted from the demands of reality by entertainment which does not demand attention either."[13]

Music is derived from the word *muse*, which means "to think." In Christian cultures, this has involved thinking and following the order and the rules of music. However, *amusement* means "not to think." In non-Christian cultures, this involves no thought about the order and rules of music but rather unashamed self-expression.

TV has been described as "chewing gum for the eyes"—a lot of motion but no nourishment. Worldly music could similarly be described as "chewing gum for the ears." It is unfortunate, but Contemporary Christian Music that incorporates worldly techniques has become "chewing gum for the soul and the emotions."

The careless musical messages of relativism and amusement lead beyond the normal need of relaxation into an escape from truth and discipline; they replace the peace that comes only from Christ and His Word with a self-centered emotional feeling. "Peace I leave with you, my peace I give unto you: not as the world giveth, give I unto you . . ." (John 14:27; see also Psalm 119:165 and Acts 10:36).

> Christianity is a demanding and serious religion. When it is delivered as easy and amusing it is a different kind of religion altogether.

Preaching Another Gospel That Is Untested by Scripture

Beware of "another gospel" presented in the music of the world. Composers are now claiming that their music is "automatically written" (psychography). An automatic writer is someone who, while in an unconscious state, writes books or music of which he has no previous knowledge. [14] Musicians must give themselves over to occult spirits to write this type of music. Channeling is communication through transcendental meditation (TM) with spirit masters, which is similar to demonic activity practiced in some religions. [15]

New Age music with its ambient sound has the explicit purpose of aiding meditation and relaxation. It also aids musicians who believe in verbal revelation. This belief is the idea that God speaks directly to people today—apart from the Bible. However, God says, "For I testify unto every man that heareth the words of the prophecy of this book, If any man shall add unto these things, God shall add unto him the plagues that are written in this book" (Revelation 22:18). This is also the message of the Old Testament: "To the law and to the testimony: if they speak not according to this word, it is because there is no light in them" (Isaiah 8:20; see also Deuteronomy 4:2).

It is our responsibility to test the spirits: "Beloved, believe not every spirit, but try the spirits whether they are of God: because many false prophets are gone out into the world" (I John 4:1). We don't judge others' intents, but we do judge if the messages in their words and the messages in their music are right or wrong compared to God's revelation of Himself in Scripture.

When the Apostle Paul said, "Beware lest any man spoil you through philosophy and vain deceit . . ." (Colossians 2:8), he was speaking to believers in the church at Colosse. Therefore, believers must be aware of channeling, verbal revelation, and automatically written music. These rudiments of the world and variations of them must not make their way into Christian music.

In his sermon titled "The Doctrine of Inspiration," John MacArthur tells of one Christian composer who said, "To dissect the song would be tampering with the inspiration of the Holy Spirit who inspired the song."[16] In the video series titled *The Language of Music*, Frank Garlock identified a composer who said, "God used a man like Paul to write the Bible; He's using me to write the songs."[17]

> Paul praised those who dissected his message.

A pastor may be inspired to preach a sermon and a musician inspired to write a song, but neither of these have the same authority as the direct inspiration of the Holy Scriptures. Paul praised those who dissected his message: "These were more noble than those in Thessalonica, in that they received the word with all readiness of mind, and searched the scriptures daily, whether those things were so" (Acts 17:11). Just as we should verify the verbal message in a sermon, so we should verify the musical message in a song.

The church at Ephesus was commended by Christ for testing ". . . them which say they are apostles, and are not, and hast found them liars" (Revelation 2:2). To refuse to examine a sermon or a song in the light of Scripture is to walk in darkness:

"For every one that doeth evil hateth the light, neither cometh to the light, lest his deeds should be reproved. But he that doeth truth cometh to the light, that his deeds may be made manifest, that they are wrought in God" (John 3:20–21).

Making Evil Acceptable Through Association

Beware of the methods used in music of the world. For purposes of occult dominion, the mind must be rendered passive so that the New Age philosophy can be injected. New Age music uses excessive repetition and polyrhythms, which go against each other to create confusion in the mind, for hypnotic induction to open up the mind to vain philosophies.

In the video series titled *The Language of Music*, Frank Garlock identified a pastor loved the music of a popular song so much that he accepted the words of the song along with the music, even when it was pointed out to him that the words were untrue. This technique could be called the technique of association. The music was so pleasing and acceptable that the false doctrine attached to it was easily accepted as well.

The same technique is taking place with TV. The false doctrine in some cartoons is made more acceptable through the appeal of flashing colors, constant motion, and unclean music.

An example of music being used to make evil acceptable is the disco group Village People, which targets "disco's primarily gay audience by featuring stereotypical gay fantasy personas."[18] The sodomite lifestyle is made more acceptable by its association with the popular, unclean musical style that often is used to promote it.

Another method of making evil acceptable through association is the use of nature sounds in some New Age music. The emphasis on nature creates an atmosphere of familiarity in order to draw listeners into the music, but then, as crossover music does, introduces listeners to the eerie and absurd. God created nature, and nature sounds can be pleasant and relaxing. However, our delight in creation must neither replace nor compete with our delight in our Creator. Mixing nature sounds with New Age musical sounds in an effort to find the peace and comfort that only God can give makes an idol of this style of music.

> New Age music uses excessive repetition and polyrhythms . . . for hypnotic induction to open up the mind to vain philosophies.

False philosophies lead us to get in touch with nature or with ourselves. Scripture warns of this danger: "Who changed the truth of God into a lie, and worshipped and served the creature more than the Creator, who is blessed for ever. Amen" (Romans 1:25). God desires for us to get in touch with Him: "Come unto me, all ye that labor and are heavy laden, and I will give you rest" (Matthew 11:28).

Teaching Self-Expression That Leads to Vain Worship

Beware of the lyrics in the music of the world. The spoken messages in modern writings must be examined.

Neo-orthodox philosophy states that the ultimate expression is self-expression. In religion it leads to the conclusion that worship is an empowering act for man. In a worship experience, the false measure of success is how good one feels.

When Abraham went up with Isaac to worship, it was not an act of self-expression. (See Genesis 22:5.) It was not an act that made Abraham feel good. It was an act of obedience and surrender to the Lord.

Christianity is a religion of sacrifice, not entertainment: "I beseech you therefore, brethren, by the mercies of God, that ye present your bodies a living sacrifice, holy, acceptable unto God, which is your reasonable service" (Romans 12:1). "But in vain they do worship me, teaching for doctrines the commandments of men" (Matthew 15:9).

Satan cannot create; all he can do is pervert. Misinformation—not lack of information—creates an illusion of knowing something but instead leads one away from truth. The more one moves into a false religion or a worldly lifestyle, the harder it will be to return to the truth.

If someone has been heavily involved in worldly music, the harder it will be for him to distinguish godly music from worldly music, because his spiritual sensitivity toward music has been dulled: "And I, brethren, could not speak unto you as unto spiritual, but as unto carnal, even as unto babes in Christ. I have fed you with milk, and not with meat: for hitherto ye were not able to bear it, neither yet now are ye able. For ye are yet carnal:

> False philosophies lead us to get in touch with nature or with ourselves. . . . God desires for us to get in touch with Him.

for whereas there is among you envying, and strife, and divisions, are ye not carnal, and walk as men?" (I Corinthians 3:1–3). In Chapter 10 we will discuss techniques Satan uses to bring destruction through music.

Nevertheless, where sin abounds, grace does much more abound. (See Romans 5:20.) Chapter 11 of this book will present some practical ideas to help those who have a desire to renew their spirits and minds. (See Ephesians 4:17–24.)

ENDNOTES: SECTION III

Chapter 8

1   Michael Ventura, "Hear That Long Snake Moan," *Whole Earth Review*, Spring 1987, p. 32

2   www.altreligion.about.com/od/symbols/ig/Vodoun-Veves/Legba.htm

3   www.paralumun.com/voodoo.htm, www.r.hodges.home.comcast.net/~r.hodges/Ear.html, and Richard Hodges, "Drum is the Ear of God," *Material for Thought*, No. 13, Far West Press, San Francisco, 1992

4   David Tame, "The Secret Power of Music," *Destiny Books*, Rochester, VT, 1984, pp. 189—190

5   Michael Ventura, "Hear That Long Snake Moan," *Whole Earth Review*, Spring 1987, p. 32

6   Michael Ventura, "Hear That Long Snake Moan," *Whole Earth Review*, Spring 1987, pp. 34—36

7   Michael Ventura, "Hear That Long Snake Moan," *Whole Earth Review*, Spring 1987, pp. 34—36

8   Martha Bayles, "Hole in our Soul," *University of Chicago Press* 1994, p. 21

9   www.nola.com/books/index.ssf/2012/04/lawrence_powell_packed_his_new.html

10 Michael Ventura, "Hear That Long Snake Moan," *Whole Earth Review*, Spring 1987, p. 36, and David Tame, "The Secret Power of Music," *Destiny Books*, Rochester, VT, 1984 p. 190

11 Michael Ventura, "Hear That Long Snake Moan," *Whole Earth Review*, Spring 1987, p. 37

12 Michael Ventura, "Hear That Long Snake Moan," *Whole Earth Review*, Spring 1987, p. 38

13 Leonard J. Seidel, "Face the Music," *Grace Unlimited Publications*, Springfield, VA, 1988 p. 36

14 www.chicago724.blogspot.com/2011/02/fyi-sushisamba-rio-celebrates-carnaval.html

15 Leonard J. Seidel, "Face the Music," *Grace Unlimited Publications*, Springfield, VA, 1988 p. 40

16 Michael Ventura, "Hear That Long Snake Moan," *Whole Earth Review*, Spring 1987, p. 42

17 www.en.wikipedia.org/wiki/Blue_Devils and www.en.wikipedia.org/wiki/Blues

18 Martha Bayles, "Hole in our Soul," *University of Chicago Press* 1994, p. 188

19 Stephen Barnard, *Rock: An Illustrated History*

20 www.sermonindex.net/modules/newbb/viewtopic.php?topic_id=27436&forum=35&start=220&viewmode=flat&order=0

21 Michael Ventura, "Hear That Long Snake Moan," *Whole Earth Review*, Summer 1987, pp. 83—84

22 David Tame, "The Secret Power of Music," *Destiny Books*, Rochester, VT, 1984, p. 192

23 www.allmusic.com/artist/al-jolson-p6841

24 www.en.wikipedia.org/wiki/Al_Jolson#cite_note-Dix-3

25 www.pbs.org/jazz/time/time_roaring.htm

26 www.dukeellington.com/ellingtonbio.html

27 www.encyclopedia.com/topic/Jerry_Lee_Lewis.aspx

28 www.refspace.com/quotes/Elvis_Presley/d:1

29 www.refspace.com/quotes/Elvis_Presley/d:1

30 www.refspace.com/quotes/Elvis_Presley/d:1

31 "Go, Cat Go", an article occasioned by Elvis' death, *New York Daily News* August 9, 1987

32 Michael Ventura, "Hear That Long Snake Moan," *Whole Earth Review*, Summer 1987, p. 90

33 Michael Ventura, "Hear That Long Snake Moan," *Whole Earth Review*, Summer 1987, p. 90

34 www.home.intekom.com/restore/History_Recording.html

35 www.sundaylaw.net/studies/truelife/music/rockmusc.htm

36 www.creators.com/conservative/brent-bozell/profanity-and-pop-music.html

Chapter 9

1 Francis A. Schaeffer, "Escape From Reason," *Inter-Varsity Press* 1974, p. 80

2 Francis A. Schaeffer, "Escape From Reason," *Inter-Varsity Press* 1974, p. 53

3 Francis A. Schaeffer, "Escape From Reason," *Inter-Varsity Press* 1974, p. 59

4 Francis A. Schaeffer, "Escape From Reason," *Inter-Varsity Press* 1974, p. 61

5 Francis A. Schaeffer, "Escape From Reason," *Inter-Varsity Press* 1974, p. 66

6 Francis A. Schaeffer, "Escape From Reason," *Inter-Varsity Press* 1974, p. 57

7 Francis A. Schaeffer, "Escape From Reason," *Inter-Varsity Press* 1974, pp. 78–79

8 Francis A. Schaeffer, "Escape From Reason," *Inter-Varsity Press* 1974, p. 56

9 www.en.allexperts.com/q/Acting-Plays-Singing-695/Audition-song-Godspell.htm

10 www.en.wikipedia.org/wiki/New_Age_music

11 www.scienceandfaith.com/Investigating_Truth.htm

12 Neil Postman, "Amusing Ourselves to Death," *Penguin Books*, 2006, p. 121

13 www.icce.rug.nl/~soundscapes/DATABASES/SWA/On_popular_music_3.shtml

14 www.en.wikipedia.org/wiki/Automatic_writing

15 www.anunseenworld.com/channelingspirits.html

16 www.gty.org/resources/sermons/90-324/The-Doctrine-of-Inspiration-Explained

17 Documented by Frank Garlock, The Language of Music video series, "The Gospel of Music," *Majesty Music* 1992

18 www.lyricsfreak.com/v/village+people/biography.html

SECTION **IV**

Significance of Music

IN THIS SECTION we will consider the power of music to destroy and the power of music to revive.

A Prayer for God's Perspective

"And it shall come to pass,
when all these things are come upon thee,
the blessing and the curse, which I have set before thee,
and thou shalt call them to mind among all the nations,
whither the LORD thy God hath driven thee,
and shalt return unto the LORD thy God,
and shalt obey his voice according to all
that I command thee this day,
thou and thy children, with all thine heart,
and with all thy soul; that then the LORD thy God
will turn thy captivity, and have compassion upon thee,
and will return and gather thee from all the nations,
whither the LORD thy God hath scattered thee"
(Deuteronomy 30:1–3)

CHAPTER 10

Satan Can Use Unclean Music to Destroy

"THE THIEF COMETH NOT, but for to steal, and to kill, and to destroy: I am come that they might have life, and that they might have it more abundantly" (John 10:10).

1. UNCLEAN MUSIC DESTROYS THE BODY

The following report is by Verle L. Bell, M.D., Psychiatrist; Pastor, St. Paul Bible Church, Chicago, Illinois:

One of the most powerfully addicting substances is something we carry with us in our own bodies. It is our adrenaline. When this substance is "used" under the circumstances God intended, it is lifesaving and causes no urge to re-indulge. However, we are able to "control" the release of this substance by choosing various activities which our defense mechanisms interpret as dangerous.

Have you ever wondered why people pay such enormous sums of money to bungee-jump or to play video games excessively? When we choose to place ourselves under simulated attack situations, our bodies move into the "fight-or-flight" response, releasing adrenaline into the blood.

The heart pounds, eyes dilate, thoughts race, breathing quickens, muscles tense, and blood is shifted to the muscles. We are now ready to fight for our lives or run desperately for shelter. However, there is no one to fight or to run from. This situation causes a "high" that feels exhilarating as long as we believe ourselves to be in control.

This sense of control is the great lie of addictions. The god we create and control to give us a sense of worth, strength, and security turns on us. The servant god becomes a monster which overpowers us.

I have seen addictions to adrenaline in veterans who turned to crime to repeat the "highs" they had learned to enjoy in Vietnam. Others steal what they do not need, start fights over any protest, drive recklessly, etc.

One of the most powerful releases of the flight-or-flight adrenaline high is music which is discordant in its beat or chords. Good music follows exact mathematical rules, which cause the mind to feel comforted, encouraged, and "safe." Musicians have found that when they go against these rules, the listener experiences an addicting high.

Like unscrupulous "diet" doctors who addicted their clients to amphetamines to ensure their continued dependence, musicians know that discordant music sells and sells. As in all addictions, victims become tolerant. The same music that once created a pleasant tingle of excitement no longer satisfies. The music becomes more jarring, louder, and more discordant. One starts with soft rock, then rock 'n' roll, then on up to heavy metal music.

With the teens and adults I have worked with, I find music addiction to be far more entrenched than alcohol or cocaine. I think this is in part due to society's acceptance of this behavior. . . .

Another characteristic of addiction is its power to consume one's time and attention. They never ask what good is being displaced by the music. I have never known a person who listens to such music to regularly fast or pray. They never share verses they have memorized. They may show emotional affirmation of God, yet have no will for personal discipline. . . . [Recall from Chapter 4 how the rhythm says, "do what you want to do," leading to self-indulgence and away from spiritual disciplines.]

> "With the teens and adults I have worked with, I find music addiction to be far more entrenched than alcohol or cocaine."

Many addicts affirm that the music actually calms them and they feel better. This is similar to a nicotine addict who claims that smoking calms him . . . the cigarette seems to calm because it reduces the withdrawal temporarily. . . . It is the same with the music. Adrenaline addicts go into withdrawal or become immersed in the available music. Then they get some "relief" from listening, but no pleasure. [1]

A basic truth found in Ephesians 5:18 is that we should not be under the control of any addictive substance: "And be not drunk with wine, wherein is excess; but be filled with the Spirit." Freedom from addiction is confirmed by the presence of all the fruits of the Spirit, especially the fruit of temperance (self-control).

In contrast to God's control over us, Satan also desires to control us through the slavery of addictions: "Know ye not, that to whom ye yield yourselves servants to obey, his servants ye are to whom ye obey; whether of sin unto death, or of obedience unto righteousness?" (Romans 6:16). These are our only two options: to be servants to sin unto death or to be servants of obedience unto righteousness. Our moral choices in musical styles, as in other areas of life, are choices of either sin or obedience, and those choices will ultimately lead to either death or righteousness.

Unclean Music Can Reduce the Quality of Health

In Chapter 2 we saw the effects of worldly music on the quality of the health of animals. In the previous point Dr. Bell confirmed how music that stimulates an adrenaline rush can create an addiction in the human body.

It would be wise to consider the physical effects of these surges of adrenaline on the quality of health. In the human body, adrenaline is a hormone and a powerful force that increases the body's strength to flee in a dangerous situation or fight off an attacker. As adrenaline flows through the system, the veins and capillaries constrict to prevent profuse bleeding in case of wounds. At the same time, the coronary arteries dilate to increase blood flow and oxygen to the vital organs such as muscles, brain, and heart.

This response is designed only for emergencies. When this response is over-stimulated, the repeated surges of adrenaline can impair circulation in the extremities and produce high blood pressure, heart conditions, and a host of other problems. It takes days for our body to filter out surges of adrenaline.

Unclean Music Can Reduce Life Expectancy

On February 11, 2009, *CBS News Entertainment* reported a study published in Britain's *Journal of Epidemiology and Community Health* that charted the lives of 1,050 American and European music artists between 1965 and 2005. The study found that rock stars are more than twice as likely to die young than the general population.

One quarter of all the musicians' deaths registered during the study period were due to drug or alcohol abuse. In the report the lead researcher, Professor Mark Bellis, called for a public health policy aimed at "preventing music icons promoting health-damaging behavior among their emulators and fans."[2]

> The root problem that links unclean music with a lifestyle of drugs and alcohol is a lack of self-control.

Note the call for restraint in professor Bellis's appeal. It is the work of the Holy Spirit to restrain evil. (See John 16:7–8). That is why believers are admonished to be controlled by the Holy Spirit and not by alcohol. (See Ephesians 5:18.)

The root problem that links unclean music with a lifestyle of drugs and alcohol is a lack of self-control. The musical message of the excessive, dominant rhythm defined in Chapter 5 is to let yourself go and to do what you want to do.

The direct effects of the unclean music and the lifestyle associated with worldly music contribute to a premature death. "My son, forget not my law; but let thine heart keep my commandments: For length of days, and long life, and peace, shall they add to thee" (Proverbs 3:1–2).

2. UNCLEAN MUSIC DISTURBS THE SOUL

We must never confuse an adrenaline rush with the filling of the Holy Spirit. The filling of the Holy Spirit begins with the filling of the Word of Christ and results in a Christlike, musical expression and Christlike character and living.

Note the parallels in the following two passages of Scripture. The first passage says: "And be not drunk with wine, wherein is excess; but be filled with the Spirit; speaking to yourselves in psalms and hymns and spiritual songs, singing and making melody in your heart to the Lord" (Ephesians 5:18–19). The second passage says: "Let the word of Christ dwell in you richly in all wisdom; teaching and admonishing one another in psalms and hymns and spiritual songs, singing with grace in your hearts to the Lord" (Colossians 3:16).

In the first passage we are to be "filled with the Spirit," which parallels the phrase "letting the word of Christ dwell in us richly" in the second passage. The equivalent of being filled with the Holy Spirit is letting the Word of Christ dwell in us richly. Note that God's Holy Spirit, Who inspired the Scriptures, will always be in agreement with the Word of Christ. The Word of Christ is the Scriptures, which testify of Him: "Search the scriptures; for in them ye think ye have eternal life: and they are they which testify of me" (John 5:39). The result of being filled with the Spirit and the Word is "speaking to yourselves in psalms," which parallels "teaching and admonishing one another in psalms" in the second passage.

One criterion for evaluating the degree to which the Holy Spirit and Word of Christ are dwelling in us richly would be the ability to trace life's problems to Biblical solutions. God's Word is the final authority in all matters of life and practice. So, if God's truth is dwelling in us richly, we will have changed lives and will be able to offer lasting answers to problems related to personal struggles, marriage conflicts, parenting challenges, financial pressures, and all other social, political, and economic issues. Of the many solutions being put forth in answer to the problems in our culture, how many of them are based on the solid teaching of Scripture? (See II Timothy 2:15.)

True happiness in the soul of an individual is a personal gift of God's grace. It occurs when that person's soul is surrendered to their spirit. Note how David directed his soul to the Lord: "Why art thou cast down, O my soul? and why art thou disquieted within me? hope thou in God: for I shall yet praise him, who is the health of my countenance, and my God" (Psalm 42:11).

> We must never confuse an adrenaline rush with the filling of the Holy Spirit.

In preparation for giving account of our souls to God, each of us must be careful to never delight more in activities such as church attendance, Scripture memory, or music than we delight in Christ Himself. "Thou wilt show me the path of life: in thy presence is fulness of joy; at thy right hand there are pleasures for evermore" (Psalm 16:11). "Rejoice in the Lord alway: and again I say, Rejoice" (Philippians 4:4).

Satan is a deceiver, and he will tempt us to pursue a variety of activities as a means of escape from the trials of life. True fulfillment in our soul cannot be gained by merely escaping from difficulties and suffering but rather true fulfillment can be gained as we experience God's power in the midst of those challenges: "Strengthened with all might, according to his glorious power, unto all patience and longsuffering with joyfulness" (Colossians 1:11).

We must never put our mind, our emotions, or our will above the truth of God's Word in our spirit.

Don't Put Your Mind Above Your Spirit

The natural thoughts of a person's mind are typically opposite to the thoughts of God's mind: "For my thoughts are not your thoughts, neither are your ways my ways, saith the LORD. For as the heavens are higher than the earth, so are my ways higher than your ways, and my thoughts than your thoughts" (Isaiah 55:8–9). Rationalization is placing the thoughts in our mind above the truth in our spirit. When we place more value on our thoughts than on God's thoughts we quench the Holy Spirit in our spirit, and the resulting tension will disturb the peace in our soul.

> Rationalization is placing the thoughts in our mind above the truth in our spirit.

The following example of overcoming the rationalization of "Christian rock" is supported by Friedrich Blume, professor of Musicology:[3]

"One of the rationalizations we previously used to justify 'Christian rock' was, 'What about Martin Luther? He used the secular music of his day, so why can't we do the same?' This rationalization breaks down under both logic and research:

- "As believers, we are to pattern our lives after Christ, not after men. Jesus warned, "How can ye believe, which receive honor one of another, and seek not the honor that cometh from God only?" (John 5:44).

- "The folk music of Martin Luther's day was melodious. Therefore, to use this as an analogy is not only inaccurate but also deceptive.

- "Much of the folk music from which Martin Luther drew his melodies was religious folk music of the pre-Reformation period. Some of these songs had been sung as early as the ninth century.

- "Of the melodies in Martin Luther's 37 chorales, 15 were composed by Martin Luther himself, 13 came from Latin hymns, 4 were from German religious folk songs, two had originally been religious pilgrim songs, two were of unknown origin, and only one came directly from a secular folk song.

  "The one secular song came from a popular song, 'I Arrived From an Alien Country' and was first used in a choral as a melody for Martin Luther's famous Christmas hymn for children, 'From Heaven on High, I Come to You.'

  "This song appeared in Martin Luther's first hymnal in 1535 but was replaced by an original tune in his 1539 hymnal. Historians believe that Martin Luther discarded the secular tune after only a short time because of people's associating it with its previous words.

- "The goal of Martin Luther in music was to replace the world's music, not to duplicate it. He used four-part harmony because he wanted to attract youth away from the world's songs."

Another rationalization used to justify "Christian rock" is, "How can this music be wrong if it is used to reach the lost?" The deception in this justification lies in the use of the term *music*.

Yes, moral music may be used for such a purpose. However, to use immoral music for such a purpose would be like asking, "How can robbing a bank be wrong if it is done to feed a family?" It is a good desire to feed a family, but it is morally wrong to rob a bank to do so.

The ends do not justify the means. Neither should we use worldly music that is inconsistent with the will of God in order to reach the lost according to His will.

An individual listening to the words of a "Christian rock" song may hear the gospel message in the lyrics, be convicted by the Holy Spirit, repent, and be saved. But his salvation experience through the message in the lyrics does not justify the evil music associated with the lyrics. Evil music that is contrary to God's nature must be changed to conform to God's nature before it can be good.

Also, if the message in the music of that song is carnal, the new convert will get two messages: a verbal message of holiness (Christ) and a musical message of worldliness (a false Christ). This produces double-mindedness, and a double-minded man is unstable in all his ways. (See James 1:8.)

Many new Christians today lack the power of self-control that is needed to conquer habits. Many other believers are quenching the Holy Spirit and thus lack power to live the victorious life of Christ day in and day out in such a way as to attract family, friends, and non-believers to the truth.

Still another problem with this rationalization of the use of Christian rock music in the church is that innocent young people in the Church hear this type of message and are drawn into a worldly lifestyle. Consider the testimony of one young lady who vividly remembers her first impression of rock music and how it gained a hold on her mind:

> "The goal of Martin Luther in music was to replace the world's music, not to duplicate it."

As a child of ten years, I remember my classmates playing this music during church and turning up the volume as loud as possible whenever the teacher left the room. The music was repulsive to me. They asked me why I didn't like it and laughed at me because I was different.

It wasn't hard to be different until my close friend began to play the music—someone I looked up to. On one occasion the music began to bother me so much that I asked her to please turn it off. This request resulted in tears, arguments, and accusations of my being a "goody-goody."

A few years later, I began dating a young man who liked rock music. He introduced me to contemporary Christian music, and I was curious. The words interested me, even though the music did not seem that great.

Another friend had me listen to some of her Christian tapes. The lyrics were clever, so I did not pay much attention to the music, but I just listened with her, trying to catch the words.

However, I did not realize what was really happening. I had attended several contemporary Christian concerts, and I remember one point when the music had a particularly dominant rock beat, the whole audience stood up, clapping with the music.

I had a strange sense of wanting to participate and at the same time wanting only to observe what was going on. I felt foolish to be part of this music. My friend and I at first refused to follow the crowd, but everyone was doing it, and it seemed awkward to be the only ones sitting. Eventually, we joined in.

I began to listen to a Christian radio show late at night which played heavy Christian rock music. The music was still repulsive to me, but I was curious. Of course, I only turned it on after my parents went to bed.

Soon after this, I got a job where they played secular rock music all day long. I did not even think of asking them to turn it off. In fact, I thought I was not being affected by the rock music. I thought music was something I could control in my own mind. At the same time I wondered why I felt so far from God and confused in my spiritual walk.

God used my parents to begin to show me that I should not listen to music which did not bring my heart closer to the Lord. I stopped listening to contemporary Christian music out of obedience, but I did not feel it had affected me that much. I did not correlate the new hunger and thirst I had for God with my recent obedience.

Months later, after "fasting" from the music, I heard some of the songs to which I had previously listened, and I was shocked by the worldly sound and felt sick inside.

I had not realized the anesthetic properties of the rock beat. I had been introduced to it a little at a time, and my spirit was also dulled a little at a time, until I could no longer distinguish music that had pleased God from that which was in rebellion against the purity of his Spirit. [4]

Don't Put Your Emotions Above Your Spirit

It is easy to place the desires of our emotions above the truth in our spirit. Just as with our thoughts, if we place more value on our emotional desires than on God's emotional desires we will quench the Holy Spirit in our spirit, and the resulting tension will disturb the peace in our soul.

Beware of the deception of soul worship. When Israel had become careless in their worship, they defended their luxurious passion for music by referring to orderly music that David had properly added to worship. They were wrong in their justification, and God sent Amos to correct them. (See Amos 5:21–6:6.)

They were wrong in what they were adding, because what they were adding was careless, excessive, and inconsistent with God's nature. They crossed over from liberty and moved into license, which is lack of restraint. "For, brethren, ye have been called unto liberty; only use not liberty for an occasion to the flesh, but by love serve one another" (Galatians 5:13).

Because music is a language of the emotions, an emotional experience can easily become confused with a spiritual experience. Soul worship is an experience with the limited energy of the human soul. Spirit worship is an experience with the true nature of God. If worldly music is mixed with spiritual worship and is pursued for personal gratification with an entertainment format, the music becomes dominant and eventually idolized. When this occurs, one can come to the point of worshipping his praise and praising his worship.

> If worldly music is mixed with spiritual worship, . . . the music becomes dominant and eventually idolized.

Beware of the delusion of foolishness. Scripture speaks of the song of fools: "It is better to hear the rebuke of the wise, than for a man to hear the song of fools" (Ecclesiastes 7:5). The contrast in this verse is between wisdom and foolishness, between that which is of God and that which is vain, hollow, or empty.

Foolishness is a deception of the devil that something bad is good, that something distorted, painful, or sad is emotionally funny. Just as humor may be a vain attempt to mask emotional pain, so foolish music that is void of the substance of God's nature offers a vain attempt to escape the emotional pain of unmet needs. Godly music includes teaching and admonishing. (See Colossians 3:16.) For this teaching and admonishing to be an expression of God's grace, it needs to occur in the structure of the music as well as in the lyrics.

Beware of the damage of sensuality. The hypnotic effect of excessive repetition lowers restraint and self-control, thus arousing and intensifying sensuality. Young men are commanded to flee youthful lusts: "Flee also youthful lusts: but follow righteousness, faith, charity, peace, with them that call on the Lord out of a pure heart" (II Timothy 2:22). Therefore, it is damaging to God's kingdom to introduce worldly music to young men and women who are seeking a pure heart.

Beware of the deception of association. It is easy to develop a strong emotional attachment to music. If Christian lyrics are added to unclean music, the lyrics will not make the music clean; however, by their association with the music, the lyrics will make the music appear to be acceptable. This is a violation of the following command: "Prove all things; hold fast that which is good. Abstain from all appearance of evil" (I Thessalonians 5:21–22).

As unclean music with Christian lyrics becomes more and more acceptable, then, by the principle of association, unclean music with secular lyrics becomes more and more acceptable. Unfortunately, the testimony of many is that after listening to and accepting "Christian rock," they soon find themselves drawn to the "real thing."

Don't Put Your Will Above Your Spirit

Scripture warns us not to harden our hearts: "Harden not your heart, as in the provocation, as in the day of temptation in the wilderness" (Psalm 95:8). It is easy to place the force of our will above the truth in our spirit. Just as with our thoughts and our emotions, if we place more value on the purpose of our will than on God's will, we will quench the

> It is easy to place the force of our will above the truth in our spirit.

Holy Spirit in our spirit, and the resulting tension will disturb the peace in our soul.

Our self-will is most evident when confronting opposing opinions. In confronting controversial issues we must purpose to heed Paul's warning: "Looking diligently lest any man fail of the grace of God; lest any root of bitterness springing up trouble you, and thereby many be defiled" (Hebrews 12:15). The following factors will help us to keep our will submitted to God's will as we engage in the spiritual warfare of identifying and removing unclean music:

- Recognize that our brothers and sisters in Christ are not our enemies: "For we wrestle not against flesh and blood, but against principalities, against powers, against the rulers of the darkness of this world, against spiritual wickedness in high places" (Ephesians 6:12).

- Actively listen to the heart, motives, and intents as well as to the words of others: "Wherefore, my beloved brethren, let every man be swift to hear, slow to speak, slow to wrath: For the wrath of man worketh not the righteousness of God" (James 1:19–20).

- Welcome criticism as a means to deepen our life message by viewing others as instruments in God's hands and by being a willing learner: "Iron sharpeneth iron; so a man sharpeneth the countenance of his friend" (Proverbs 27:17).

- Don't focus on being "right" or "wrong," but rather focus on what is Biblical. Give Scriptural passages and principles and ask others for them. Another way of saying this is to not focus on what I like or think but rather to focus on what God is like: "These were more noble than those in Thessalonica, in that they received the word with all readiness of mind, and searched the scriptures daily, whether those things were so" (Acts 17:11).

Not all conflicts or differences of opinion will be resolved immediately. There will be areas about which we may have to agree to disagree. Other areas will need to be pursued with future study. Hopefully there will be understanding as the nature of music is held up to the nature of God Himself as revealed in the Scriptures. There were three different types of re-

> There were three different types of responses to Paul's teaching . . .

sponses to Paul's teaching: "And when they heard of the resurrection of the dead, some mocked: and others said, We will hear thee again of this matter. So Paul departed from among them. Howbeit certain men clave unto him, and believed" (Acts 17:32–34).

3. UNCLEAN MUSIC INVITES THE PRESENCE OF EVIL SPIRITS

"Be sober, be vigilant [in evaluating our music]; because your adversary the devil, as a roaring lion, walketh about, seeking whom he may devour" (I Peter 5:8).

Consider the testimony of a Christian from Zimbabwe who had formerly been involved in demonic activities:

I am very sensitive to the beat in music, because when I was a boy, I played the drums in our village worship rituals. The beat that I played on the drum was to get the demon spirits into people. When I became a Christian, I rejected this kind of beat because I realized how damaging it was. When I turned on a Christian radio station in the United States, I was shocked. The beat that I used to play to call up the evil spirits is in the music I heard on the Christian station. [5]

Consider the testimony of one who left heathen practices:

It was in the early 1970s when my sisters arrived in Kalimantan, Karat, Indonesia, where our parents were serving as missionaries. My sisters had brought to the mission field a contemporary Christian record which they said was the "in" thing back home. They were playing the record one evening when an older national Christian came to the door. To my sisters' astonishment, his immediate question was, "Why are you playing witch doctors' music and calling on Satan?" This Christian had left the old heathen practices, which included calling on evil spirits. He recognized the "Christian music" as the same kind of music that the witch doctors used. [6]

Consider the testimony of one who served as a missionary. In the book *Peace Child*, missionary Don Richardson discovered a redemptive analogy in the culture of a western New Guinea tribe which opened that tribe to Christ. He writes his book to share his belief that every society has a redemptive analogy, so his book is not a book about music. However, on pages 71–72 he records the following observation of the use of music in the Sawi tribe:

Occasionally the sudden increase in the tempo of the drums would trigger a climax of wild exultant shouting. Out of the midst of each resounding tumult a single warrior would raise his voice to a high pitch and scream in rapid oratorical Sawi the details of a murder he had committed. The others would suddenly fall silent to listen. The speaker would then complete the story in five or six sentences, leaping straight up and down with spear poised, tossing his head from side to side. At the conclusion of his oration the entire assembly would break forth into shouting again, in commemoration of the slaying described. Then the drums would resume their ominous booming, portraying the long intervals of plotting and waiting, which separate realizations of glorious treachery. Five, six, or seven minutes later, the drums would trigger still another outburst of glory to conceive and bring to birth still another warrior's shrill boast of bloodthirstiness. . . .

The chanting itself consisted entirely of nonsense syllables. The Sawi never used music to convey a message; they used it only to impress the senses. For them the medium [music] was the message.

Consider the testimony of a secular musician. Little Richard, an American singer, songwriter, pianist and recording artist, is considered key in the transition from rhythm and blues to rock and roll in the 1950s. He readily admits:

I believe this kind of music is demonic. . . . A lot of the beats in music today are taken from voodoo, from the voodoo drums.[7]

From the drums of Tophet (see Chapter 4 of this book) to the drums of African tribal worship (see Chapter 8) to the drums of Indonesia and New Guinea to the drums of the cities and churches of the United States, Satan uses the rhythm in music to excite the sensual drives of our fleshly carnal nature. This is in defiance of God's rightful control in the human heart and opens mankind to Satan's influence and control.

To be effective for the kingdom of God and His righteousness, we must be alert to the various ways Satan is walking about, seeking whom he may devour in the United States.

4. SATAN CAN MAKE HIMSELF APPEAR AS LIGHT

God is described as being in the light: "Who coverest thyself with light as with a garment: who stretchest out the heavens like a curtain" (Psalm 104:2). "But if we walk in the light, as he is in the light, we have fellowship one with another, and the blood of Jesus Christ his Son cleanseth us from all sin" (I John 1:7).

Satan is most often pictured in darkness and as being wicked. However, he is capable of transforming himself to appear in light as being beautiful and attractive: "For such are false apostles, deceitful workers, transforming themselves into the apostles of Christ. And no marvel; for Satan himself is transformed into an angel of light" (II Corinthians 11:13–14). What appears to be light is not always light. What appears to be light may actually be darkness in disguise.

> What appears to be light may actually be darkness in disguise.

Why would Satan do this? Obviously, so that he can move around in Christian circles undetected. "Beware of false prophets, which come to you in sheep's clothing, but inwardly they are ravening wolves" (Matthew 7:15).

Because musical sounds are moral, they will be good or evil. They may appear to be light but are actually darkness. Based on the way Satan can appear, it is all the more imperative that we create a gap between godly music and worldly music, not just draw a thin line of separation.

> Israel mixed heathen elements with their worship and brought the judgment of God upon themselves.

Christians who listen to contemporary music with the worldly beat may be sincere, but they are sincerely wrong because the music is inconsistent with God's nature, His will, and His design. To worship God in Spirit includes sincerity, but for worship to be acceptable to God we must worship God "in spirit and in truth" (John 4: 23–24).

Israel mixed heathen elements with their worship and brought the judgment of God upon themselves: "They did not destroy the nations, concerning whom the LORD commanded them: But were mingled among the heathen, and learned their works" (Psalm 106:34–35; see also Isaiah 42:8, 17, 24, and 25). Paul warned the carnal Christians at Corinth: "Your glorying is not good. Know ye not that a little leaven leaveneth the whole lump?" (I Corinthians 5:6). A little worldly beat can defile many godly words by communicating an unholy message to the young, the weak, and the unsuspecting that they can be Christians and still do what they want to do.

If one becomes a Christian in an entertainment environment, it is like a seed sown on shallow ground: he may spring up immediately, but when trials or persecution comes, then he is much more likely to fall away because his life is rooted in pleasure.

Satan is out to destroy us, and he is a master of deception. He is even able to use miracles as a means of deception. (See Revelation 13:11–14, 16:14, and 19:20.) Let's not be ignorant of his devices: "Lest Satan should get an advantage of us: for we are not ignorant of his devices" (II Corinthians 2:11).

5. THE HOLY SPIRIT CAN USE CLEAN MUSIC TO OVERPOWER EVIL SPIRITS

The Bible records that the right kind of melodious music can drive away evil spirits: "But the spirit of the LORD departed from Saul, and an evil spirit from the LORD troubled him. And Saul's servants said unto him, Behold now, an evil spirit from God troubleth thee. Let our lord now command thy servants, which are before thee, to seek out a man, who is a cunning player on an harp: and it shall come to pass, when the evil spirit from God is upon thee, that he shall play with his hand, and thou shalt be well" (I Samuel 16:14–16). As God removed the influence of the Holy Spirit from Saul's life, He permitted an evil spirit to influence Saul. Saul's servants recognized the power of godly music to overpower this evil spirit: "And it came to pass, when the evil spirit from God was upon Saul, that David took an harp, and played with his hand: so Saul was refreshed, and was well, and the evil spirit departed from him" (I Samuel 16:23). We have seen how unclean music can attract evil spirits; in the same way, godly music can drive away evil spirits.

CHAPTER 11

God Can Use Clean Music to Revive

REVIVAL IS A CONTEST OF POWER. When Elijah came to the people of God he said: "How long halt ye between two opinions? if the LORD be God, follow him: but if Baal, then follow him. And the people answered him not a word" (I Kings 18:21). Notice the awkward silence of the people. However, when the people saw the fire of the Lord consume the drenched sacrifice, "they fell on their faces: and they said, The LORD, he is the God; the LORD, he is the God" (I Kings 18:39).

Who will the United States worship—the God of our fathers or the god of self that is being promoted by the music of the world? As in other revivals, the citizens of the United States will follow the Lord when they see the fire of God's Spirit working in God's people and meeting needs that the world cannot meet. Some of these needs include the healing of diseases, the maintaining of marriage oneness, the turning of the hearts of parents toward their children and the turning of the hearts of children toward their parents, the fulfillment of knowing God's calling, the provision of funds, and the breaking of habits—including breaking the addiction of worldly music.

There are many battlefronts in a war. The same is true in spiritual warfare. The following ten recommendations are offered to those who desire revival on the battlefield of music.

1. LEARN TO DISCERN TRUTH ABOUT MUSIC WITH YOUR SPIRIT NOT JUST YOUR MIND

How do we resolve the conflict between two people with different music standards? Typically what occurs is the person with a lower standard (let's call this person Mr. Low) feels the person with a higher standard (let's call this person Mr. High) is "legalistic." Mr. High may in fact be legalistic, or he may in fact be experiencing the power of God's grace at work in that area of his life.

Let's assume the latter. In this case, Mr. Low would still view the standard as "legalistic" if he were feeling pressure to move up to a higher standard he did not like or could not attain. If he did not have the power of God's grace to move in this direction, then he would be relying on his own limited resources, which would make it a struggle for him. There would be no joy, no deepening relationship with Christ, and thus it would become a legalistic standard for him. The only real solution to changing a standard is the work of God's grace in the heart.

What can Mr. High do to help Mr. Low see his need for God's grace? Mr. High can give Mr. Low a different perspective by asking Mr. Low to consider one of his own godly standards: a moral standard in which Mr. Low is experiencing God's grace, in other words, a standard which, if lowered in his life, would violate his conscience.

Now Mr. High can ask Mr. Low to consider a third person (let's call this person Mr. Friend) who has a standard lower than Mr. Low's. What would Mr. Low desire for Mr. Friend? If Mr. Low's standard is truly a Biblical moral standard, then Mr. Low would desire God's grace to be poured out upon Mr. Friend so that he could experience God's best in this area of his life. Now Mr. Low can understand what Mr. High desires for him.

There is only one way to get God's grace. That is to humble ourselves. "Likewise, ye younger, submit yourselves unto the elder. Yea, all of you be subject one to another, and be clothed with humility: for God resisteth the proud, and giveth grace to the humble" (I Peter 5:5). We must all be willing to humble ourselves, to listen to what others have to say about our moral standards, and to evaluate these comments in light of God's Word. Our eyes must not be on men but rather on God and the grace He gives us to move toward Himself.

That is the approach I would ask you to use in considering the following points to discern with your spirit the truth about music.

Develop an Intimate Knowledge of God Through His Word

"O how love I thy law! it is my meditation all the day" (Psalm 119:97). "This book of the law shall not depart out of thy mouth; but thou shalt meditate therein day and night, that thou mayest observe to do according to all that is written therein: for then thou shalt make thy way prosperous, and then thou shalt have good success" (Joshua 1:8). "Let us hear the conclusion of the whole matter: Fear God, and keep his commandments: for this is the whole duty of man" (Ecclesiastes 12:13).

By what means does the Spirit of God communicate Truth to our spirit? His most obvious means is the infallible Word of God: "And take the helmet of salvation, and the sword of the Spirit, which is the word of God" (Ephesians 6:17). It is not possible for the Holy Spirit to lead us into any activity that is inconsistent with the Word of God. The Holy Spirit does not guide or speak independent of Christ, but rather He guides us into the truth that He receives from Christ: "Howbeit when he, the Spirit of truth, is come, he will guide you into all truth: for he shall not speak of himself; but whatsoever he shall hear, that shall he speak: and he will shew you things to come. He shall glorify me: for he shall receive of mine, and shall shew it unto you" (John 16:13–14). To practice a musical style that cannot be supported with Scripture is not to be led of the Spirit but rather to be presumptuous. One may be sincere, but if he is not thinking Biblically then he is sincerely presumptuous, not sincerely spiritual.

> One may be sincere, but if he is not thinking Biblically then he is sincerely presumptuous, not sincerely spiritual.

The Word of God clarifies the difference between the inclinations of our soul (mind, emotions, and will) and the inclinations of our spirit: "For the word of God is quick, and powerful, and sharper than any two-edged sword, piercing even to the dividing asunder of soul and spirit, and of the joints and marrow, and is a discerner of the thoughts and intents of the heart" (Hebrews 4:12).

How do we discern Truth? Not by the natural inclinations of our mind and emotions that we possessed even when we were unbelievers, but rather by our spirit, which is made alive at the new birth and is guided by the Holy Spirit: "But the natural man receiveth not the things of the Spirit of God: for they are foolishness unto him: neither can he know them, because they are spiritually discerned" (I Corinthians 2:14).

To spiritually discern the Truth about a topic we must search out what the Scriptures say about that topic: "These were more noble than those in Thessalonica, in that they received the word with all readiness of mind, and searched the scriptures daily, whether those things were so" (Acts 17:11). As discussed in Chapter 6, Paul needed to know the truth about the topic of a pastor's salary. He discerned the truth on this topic from a statute in the Old Testament regarding the feeding of oxen. In the same way, we bring our topics to the Scriptures looking for direct Biblical statements and for Biblical principles and analogies. Just as Paul discovered rich insights as he brought his topic up to the light of Scripture, so we can discern truth about the elements of music as we bring those elements up to the light of Scriptural passages that reveal God's nature.

An intimate knowledge of truth will automatically reveal counterfeits. People who identify counterfeit money become so familiar with real bills that they develop an extra sensitive ability to spot counterfeit bills. We don't have to be expert musicians to identify the elements of worldly music that are inconsistent with God's nature, but we do need to have a good understanding of God's nature through His living Word. We need to develop regular family devotions, maintain a daily practice of personal Bible reading and prayer, and memorize as much Scripture as possible in order for His Word to be living and active in us: "But his delight is in the law of the Lord; and in his law doth he meditate day and night. And he shall be like a tree planted by the rivers of water, that bringeth forth his fruit in his season; his leaf also shall not wither; and whatsoever he doeth shall prosper" (Psalm 1:2–3). The goal is to become so familiar with the character of God that any activity that is inconsistent with His holy nature (including the performing of worldly music) will be easily recognized.

> The process of searching the Scriptures and verifying whether a caution was indeed accurate leads to maturity.

It is possible to detect unclean music in our spirit before being capable of explaining what is technically wrong with it in our mind: "A prudent man foreseeth the evil, and hideth himself: but the simple pass on, and are punished" (Proverbs 22:3 and 27:12). Those who are born again are led by the Holy Spirit, not just by their natural inclinations: "For as many as are led by the Spirit of God, they are the sons of God" (Romans 8:14). If a believer senses in his spirit that the Holy Spirit is giving him a caution about the music he is listening to, then he should stop listening to it immediately in obedience to the Holy Spirit. He should not be as the simple, who pass on and are punished. One of the punishments for not listening to God's voice is that we harden our heart and become less sensitive in our spirit to God's Spirit. ". . . To day if ye will hear his voice, harden not your hearts, as in the provocation" (Hebrews 3:15). If a believer repeatedly hardens his heart, he can reach the state of being carnal rather than spiritual: "And I, brethren, could not speak unto you as unto spiritual, but as unto carnal, even as unto babes in Christ" (I Corinthians 3:1).

Of course any caution we believe we receive from the Holy Spirit needs to be tested against Scripture. The process of searching the Scriptures and verifying whether a caution was indeed accurate leads to maturity: "But strong meat belongeth to them that are of full age, even those who by reason of use have their senses exercised to discern both good and evil" (Hebrews 5:14). The more we exercise our spiritual senses, listen to the cautions of the Holy Spirit, and verify those cautions with Scripture, the greater will be our capacity to discern good and evil. The more our cautions prove to be Biblically accurate, the more they will lead to Biblical convictions.

We are commanded to "quench not the Spirit" (I Thessalonians 5:19). It is important to learn to listen to the cautions and promptings of the Holy Spirit, because His desire is to guide us into all truth. Many lies and much unnecessary pain and sorrow can be avoided with instant obedience to the initial promptings of the Holy Spirit. If we sense the smell of a rat, it may well be a rat. We don't have to open a sewer to know what it smells like.

Beware of Personal Preferences That Are Not Based on Biblical Principles

Many of us have had things we "liked" and allowed in our life twenty years ago. But we have matured over the years and would never allow them in our life today. How I "feel" right now about something that is not based on Scripture may well change in the next twenty years. So, we can see that absolute truth cannot be based merely on what we think or feel at the present time.

Therefore, we should not embrace a current standard that is based only on personal thoughts and feelings. Rather, our standards need to be based on Biblical principles. Are your standards in music based on personal preference or Biblical conviction?

Beware of "Blessings" That Are Not Based on Biblical Principles

Do not assume that what appears to be a "blessing" or is claimed to be a "blessing" is totally acceptable to the Lord. For example, consider the story of what happened when Moses struck the rock twice in the wilderness.

Shortly after receiving the manna, Israel murmured against Moses over a lack of water: "And the LORD said unto Moses, Go on before the people, and take with thee of the elders of Israel; and thy rod, wherewith thou smotest the river, take in thine hand, and go. Behold, I will stand before thee there upon the rock in Horeb; and thou shalt smite the rock, and there shall come water out of it, that the people may drink. And Moses did so in the sight of the elders of Israel" (Exodus 17:5–6). Moses obeyed the Lord and Israel experienced a great blessing that day.

Later, after failing to enter the Promised Land through unbelief, Israel began wandering in the desert, a journey that lasted for forty years. And again the people murmured against

Moses about a lack of water: "And the LORD spake unto Moses, saying, Take the rod, and gather thou the assembly together, thou, and Aaron thy brother, and speak ye unto the rock before their eyes; and it shall give forth his water, and thou shalt bring forth to them water out of the rock: so thou shalt give the congregation and their beasts drink. And Moses took the rod from before the LORD, as he commanded him. And Moses and Aaron gathered the congregation together before the rock, and he said unto them, Hear now, ye rebels; must we fetch you water out of this rock? And Moses lifted up his hand, and with his rod he smote the rock twice: and the water came out abundantly, and the congregation drank, and their beasts also. And the LORD spake unto Moses and Aaron, Because ye believed me not, to sanctify me in the eyes of the children of Israel, therefore ye shall not bring this congregation into the land which I have given them" (Numbers 20:7–12). Notice the consequences of Moses' actions.

> The fact that Moses was "blessed" was not an indication itself that everything that took place that day was pleasing to God.

God told Moses to speak to the rock. Moses disobeyed God's word and instead smote the rock twice. God could have chastened Moses publicly for his disobedience by withholding His power. However, in God's mercy He blessed Moses with a great miracle before the people. At the same time, in God's holiness there were consequences for Moses. The fact that he was "blessed" was not an indication itself that everything that took place that day was pleasing to God.

It is possible for God to give us what we like even though it is not what is best for us: "And he gave them their request; but sent leanness into their soul" (Psalm 106:15). "Blessings" may well be an evidence of God's approval, but not always: ". . . He maketh his sun to rise on the evil and on the good, and sendeth rain on the just and on the unjust" (Matthew 5:45). God is full of love and mercy: "He hath not dealt with us after our sins; nor rewarded us according to our iniquities" (Psalm 103:10). Just as not everything that first appears to be a curse is always a curse, so everything that first appears to be a blessing is not always God's best. When testing "fruit," we must verify that the fruit is consistent with God's nature and His will, according to His Word.

> "Blessings" may well be an evidence of God's approval, but not always.

2. GO ON A MUSIC FAST

After a careful study of the Scriptures, if you still have a struggle in making a clear distinction between clean music and unclean music, consider the following testimony about going on a music fast:

> I pressed my foot against the accelerator. The windows were rolled down, and the wind was rushing across my face. The car stereo was cranked up loud with one of my favorite Christian songs.

> "Feel the beat, feel the beat," boomed this musical command. I listened to it; I embraced it; I obeyed it.

Section IV

I loved the beat. It was my comfort in sorrow, my solace in grief, my counselor in confusion. I was willing to stand against the disapproval of my parents, my pastor, and even some of my friends in order to satisfy my desire for the beat.

This pursuit for the beat began when I was a little girl. My uncle, who is only six years older than I, would care for us while my parents were gone. He was my hero in every way. He would play "hard rock" in his car.

One afternoon we were stopped by a policeman and given a ticket because the music was so loud. My uncle's love for rock music progressed, along with rebellion, drugs, suspension from school, thievery, and a police record.

My uncle eventually moved away, but his music stayed with me. I began following in the same footsteps as my hero.

I remember the first record I bought. It had pictures of prostitutes on the front. I noticed that the album covers of my favorite songs often depicted evil things. The beat seemed to increase my thirst for evil. My clothes, my habits, and my attitudes changed to reflect the rebellion within me.

Shortly after my thirteenth birthday, my entire family responded to the message of salvation. Many changes took place as a result of our commitment to Jesus Christ. Alcohol bottles were emptied, books were burned, even my rock records and tapes were destroyed. I experienced great joy and freedom from the sins that had been controlling my life.

However, it did not take long for unresolved bitterness toward my mother to surface. I experienced anger and deep loneliness. Meanwhile it seemed as if the rock beat was popping up everywhere. I tried to resist its influence, knowing the association that it had with my habits of the past, and yet I struggled to find something to fill my void.

Then I was introduced to "Christian rock" music as a means of evangelizing my unsaved friends. I was so excited, because I could find contemporary Christian artists that sounded like my old secular favorites. At first, I started with a mild beat, for fear of getting involved with rock music again. However, I was told by many respected Christians that it was the *lyrics* that made secular music wrong, not the tune.

My old desire for "the beat" was satisfied again, but the things it required of me waged a war within my soul. It seemed as though there was always a conflict between my family and me. Thoughts of suicide came to me during this period of time. I had a deep desire to follow the Lord, yet I could not understand why I had no victory in my daily life.

I attended a seminar where I was challenged to dedicate my life to the Lord. This included yielding my rights in the areas of music, friends, and clothes. I confessed my hidden sins to my parents and asked them to forgive me of my rebellion.

I purposed to seek their counsel for my decisions. When they started talking about "my" music, I struggled to find where to draw the line between good and bad music.

The *Striving for Excellence* music course [IBLP] was presented in my Sunday school during that time. It gave examples of music that contained the rock beat. I laughed out loud as I heard these examples. I could not even hear the beat in those mild songs. Instead of having questions answered about the rock beat, I was left with more questions.

I prayerfully decided to go on a "music fast." I packed up all my questionable tapes and listened only to music that was clearly unquestionable. I began memorizing large portions of Scripture during this "music fast"— something that I had had a difficult time doing before.

Instead of falling asleep listening to music, I went to bed reciting Scripture. For the first time, I could see definite progress in my commitments to the Lord. Whenever I faced temptation, I would go to Scripture instead of my tape deck.

After the music fast, I reevaluated my music tapes and was shocked to recognize the rock beat in many songs where I had never even heard it before.

I then made it my goal to create a gap between the music to which I would listen and the music of the world, rather than seeing how close I could come to the line. This was created by taking steps to regain the "ground" in my soul that I had given to Satan through wrong music. Now I am so glad that I am finally free! [1]

A note in the book following this testimony suggests, "If you are unable to carry out a fast from worldly music for at least a month, it would confirm that you are addicted to it."

Just as fasting food cleanses our physical bodies and brings the various body systems back into balance, so a music fast for a period of one month can have the same cleansing effect in our soul. Memorize portions of Scripture during this music fast. Then, afterwards, replace any unclean-style music with godly, melodious music.

3. ASK GOD TO REGAIN SURRENDERED "GROUND" IN OUR SOUL

After being born again in our spirit there is an ongoing war for control in our soul: "Dearly beloved, I beseech you as strangers and pilgrims, abstain from fleshly lusts, which war against the soul" (I Peter 2:11). All day long our soul makes decisions as to whether we will follow the impulses of our flesh or the impulses of our spirit.

Understand How "Ground" Is Given in Our Soul

Any time we make a decision to put our own desires above what the Bible reveals about God's desires, as in listening to unclean music, we quench the Holy Spirit. "For the flesh lusteth against the Spirit, and the Spirit against the flesh: and these are contrary the one to the other: so that ye cannot do the things that ye would" (Galatians 5:17). If we fail to resolve this conflict before the sun goes down, we surrender that area of our soul to Satan: ". . . Let not the sun go down upon your wrath: Neither give place to the devil" (Ephesians 4:26–27).

In this spiritual conflict Paul warns us to "neither give place to the devil" (Ephesians 4:27). The word for *place* in the Greek is an area of legal control. If we give ground to Satan by listening to unclean music then he has the legal right to construct a stronghold, which is a false conclusion that is contrary to Scripture: "(For the weapons of our warfare are not carnal, but mighty through God to the pulling down of strong holds;) casting down imaginations, and every high thing that exalteth itself against the knowledge of God, and bringing into captivity every thought to the obedience of Christ" (II Corinthians 10:4–5). Sometimes such a conclusion is believed out of ignorance, and at other times it is constructed to justify our personal desires.

> After being born again in our spirit there is an ongoing war for control in our soul.

Take Steps to Regain "Ground"

Get alone with God and humbly confess the specific sin that quenched the Holy Spirit (see I John 1:9). Ask for forgiveness in the name and through the shed blood of the Lord Jesus Christ (see Revelation 12:11).

We are not able to take "ground" back ourselves, but God can: "He restoreth my soul: he leadeth me in the paths of righteousness for his name's sake" (Psalm 23:3). Audibly make a request, such as is stated in the following example: "God, would You take back the ground I gave to Satan with the sin of inviting unclean music into my life?"

It is God's responsibility to regain the ground we surrendered, but it is our responsibility to tear down the strongholds that Satan built on that territory: "Casting down imaginations, and every high thing that exalteth itself against the knowledge of God, and bringing into captivity every thought to the obedience of Christ" (II Corinthians 10:5). We must purpose to search out and destroy every lie and false conclusion we have accepted from Satan and then build up towers of truth in their place through daily Bible reading and memorizing, and meditating on Scripture: "Wherefore lay apart all filthiness and superfluity of naughtiness, and receive with meekness the engrafted word, which is able to save your souls" (James 1:21). David said: "Wherewithal shall a young man cleanse his way? by taking heed thereto according to thy word. With my whole heart have I sought thee: O let me not wander from thy commandments. Thy word have I hid in mine heart, that I might not sin against thee" (Psalm 119:9–11).

4. DEFINE A PERSONAL STANDARD OF EXCELLENCE

Write down your personal standard regarding music and the Scriptural basis for it. This will help you establish in your heart and mind the kind of music that is or is not acceptable to the Lord and equip you to communicate your standard to others.

Review Section I and develop a written standard regarding the morality of musical sound apart from the lyrics. Here are some suggestions in regard to the morality of music:

- Because God is holy, the music that exists in God's presence is holy and morally pure.

- Musical sound, apart from the lyrics, either expresses or contradicts God's holy character.

- For music to be acceptable it must be consistent with God's divine nature.

- The basis for music being acceptable to God is not what we like but rather what God is like.

- Individual notes are amoral, but the moment they are combined they begin to communicate moral messages.

- Because music is a "language of emotion," it is capable of bypassing the brain and directly influencing the heart.

- Music is a universal language that communicates across all cultures and all spoken languages.

- The form by which words are presented (e.g., attitudes, music) can affect the meaning of what is communicated and change the meaning of the literal words that are used.

- Only within the wide range of morally acceptable music is there room for cultural differences and personal preferences.

Review Section II and include in your standard a summary of the importance of melody, harmony, and rhythm being consistent with the nature of God. Because the spiritual nature of God can be understood in terms of the physical things He has made, it is possible to examine the melody, harmony, and rhythm of a selection of music and see where their characteristics do or do not agree with the characteristics of God's eternal power and godhead. Some specific ideas in regard to the details of music include these:

- The primary characteristics of most Contemporary Christian Music in the United States today, either secular or religious, are (1) a dominant rhythm, (2) excessive repetition, and (3) high tension. The dominant rhythm is loud, prevailing over the melody and harmony, and is usually accompanied with syncopation, highly accented backbeats, break-beats, and poly-rhythms.

- Excessive rising in the melody before any downward turn builds high tension and creates a sense of unfulfillment. Frustration arises in the listener because the rise is not resolved, the expectation does not come, and the promise is not fulfilled. However, God is faithful, and He offers resolution and fulfillment to mankind. He keeps all of His promises. He is the God of peace in the midst of frustration and anxiety.

- Excessive descending in the melody before any upward turn induces excessive relaxation and creates a sense of defeat. Despair depresses the listener because the fall is not recovered, the answer is not given, and the hope is not offered. However, when Jesus is our Savior, we have victory over sin and death. He is the God of hope in the midst of despair and defeat.

- Excessive dissonance in the harmony builds high tension through disorder and disarray. Excessive clashing of the notes or chords can distress the listener and be an influence in stirring up confusion, restlessness, alarm, and rebellion. However, the Holy Spirit is the Comforter and chaos and restlessness are not part of His being. Chord progression to the tonic home center is a picture of the ultimate goal of being united—totally—with our Heavenly Father. Because our "tonic home" is with Jesus Christ in heaven, we do not let our heart become troubled.

- Excessive consonance blends the chords in the harmony to the extent that it provides no interest in the composition. The lack of contrast relaxes the listener to the point of encouraging indifference and apathy. However, God is true and righteous and He is not indifferent toward evil for the sake of superficial oneness. He is a righteous Judge, and in His eyes there is a clear distinction between good and evil.

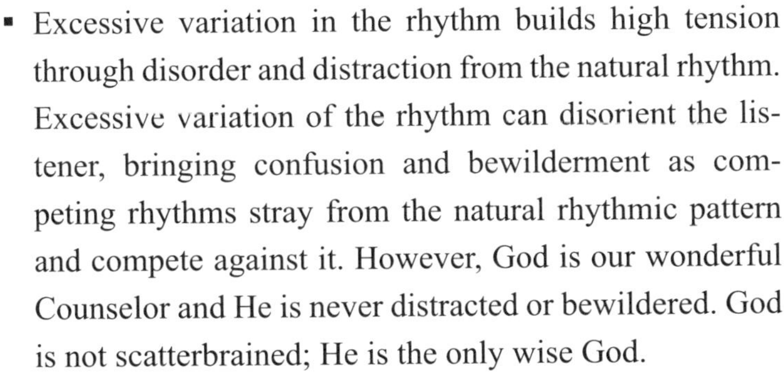

> To mix ungodly music with godly words is to be double-minded.

- Excessive variation in the rhythm builds high tension through disorder and distraction from the natural rhythm. Excessive variation of the rhythm can disorient the listener, bringing confusion and bewilderment as competing rhythms stray from the natural rhythmic pattern and compete against it. However, God is our wonderful Counselor and He is never distracted or bewildered. God is not scatterbrained; He is the only wise God.

- Excessive repetition in the rhythm tends to induce excessive relaxation. When the same rhythm is repeated excessively, without variation, the monotonous repetition of the hypnotic pattern can dull the senses to the point of tempting the listener to lower restraint and disregard self-control. However, God is love and His senses are not dull. He is alert and attentive to all of our needs. He is sovereign, in control, and actively involved in working all things together for good to them that love Him.

- Based on the command to love not the world, why would those who seek a godly lifestyle unequally yoke themselves together with a worldly musical style? To mix ungodly music with godly words is to be double-minded.

- There is a correlation between the drives of our spirit and the melody and a correlation between the drives of our body and the rhythm. If your goal is for the spiritual part of your being to be dominant, then you should evaluate whether or not the type of music you are listening to is helping you achieve this goal.

Review Section III and include in your statement the historical origins of contemporary musical sounds. Some ideas in regard to the history of music include these:

- Music is not a requirement for worship.

- There is no Biblical basis for music to take center stage the way it has taken center stage in so many "worship" services.

- Because music is a language of the emotions, an emotional experience can easily be mistaken for a spiritual experience.

- We need to clearly distinguish the difference between spiritual and secular enthusiasm.

- Biblical faith teaches denial of the body, while worldly worship is a practice that excites the body.

- We must guard against mixing a doctrine in word that denies the body (the lower sinful nature) with a practice in music that excites the body (self-expression without self-restraint).

- Satan offers many substitutes for denying oneself and the filling of the Holy Spirit, and in the process he diverts worship to himself.

- Excessive, controlling rhythm communicates a message that is in direct opposition to the gospel of Christ; it communicates a false gospel message.

- Dominant, controlling, rhythmic music did not originate in the churches in the United States, but rather it was brought in from the world with a contradictory message.

- There needs to be a process of "proving" and approving those who lead music in worship services, just as we have a process of approving those who proclaim the Word in worship services.

Below are some additional factors that will help make your standard of music a standard of excellence:

Consider Creating a Gap—Not a Line

When our family visited the Grand Canyon, we did not see how close we could walk to the edge without falling over. Most people would not see how close they could get to a rattlesnake without getting bit.

Based on the command to "abstain from all appearance of evil" (I Thessalonians 5:22) and the factors studied in Section II that define godly music, we can seek and experience God's best in music not by drawing a thin line of separation between good and evil but rather by creating a wide gap between good and evil choices.

In striving for excellence, a clear difference between the holy and the unholy, between the spiritual and the carnal, between the Christlike and the worldly can be achieved by avoiding all music that emphasizes a backbeat, break-beat, or poly-rhythms and by allowing only a minimal amount of syncopation, which may be needed to support the melody. Chapter 5 lists many other factors of worldly music, such as sliding notes, but it is primarily the rhythm that is emphasized today. "But put ye on the Lord Jesus Christ, and make not provision for the flesh, to fulfil the lusts thereof" (Romans 13:14).

Consider the "Weaker" Brother

We have established in Section I that musical sound itself is moral and can be either good or evil. However, let's consider the position of those who believe musical sound is amoral and is neither good nor evil. From their perspective it is possible to read I Corinthians 8:1–13 and equate meat with music on the assumption that both meat and music are amoral. They could classify those offended by worldly music as a "weaker" brother and conclude that it is acceptable to listen to worldly music.

If those who believe music is amoral base their belief on the I Corinthians 8:1–13 passage, then based on the conclusion of this passage they would be compelled to honor the weaker brother's music standard in order to not offend the weaker brother's conscience.

Paul emphasized the importance of not putting a stumbling block in the way of a brother's conscience by pausing in his discussion of meat offered to idols and giving a personal testimony. In Chapter 9 Paul explained his freedom as an apostle to charge a wage for his preaching services. Yet he denied himself this privilege to avoid offending those who would suspect him of preaching for personal gain. (See I Corinthians 9:14–19.)

If those who say music is amoral believe the Scriptures are truly the final authority in all matters of life and practice, then no church will accept worldly music as part of public worship when it violates the conscience of a single member due to his strong moral conviction.

The principle of not offending a "weaker" brother is not the primary reason presented in this book to establish a personal standard of

> A clear difference between the holy and the unholy . . . can be achieved by avoiding all music that emphasizes a backbeat, break-beat, or poly-rhythms.

excellence in music. The principle of not offending a "weaker" brother is simply the reason to exercise caution and self-control to avoid persisting in practices that are offensive to the standards and consciences of others.

Consider the Danger of Fellowship With Devils

Let's continue to consider the position of those who believe musical sound is amoral and is neither good nor evil. Paul resumes the topic of meat offered to idols in Chapter 10 and warns those who **think they stand** to take heed lest they fall (see I Corinthians 10:12) into the very real danger of having fellowship with devils: "Wherefore, my dearly beloved, flee from idolatry. I speak as to wise men; judge ye what I say. The cup of blessing which we bless, is it not the communion of the blood of Christ? The bread which we break, is it not the communion of the body of Christ? For we being many are one bread, and one body: for we are all partakers of that one bread. Behold Israel after the flesh: are not they which eat of the sacrifices partakers of the altar? What say I then? that the idol is any thing, or that which is offered in sacrifice to idols is any thing? But I say, that the things which the Gentiles sacrifice, they sacrifice to devils, and not to God: and **I would not that ye should have fellowship with devils**. Ye cannot drink the cup of the Lord, and the cup of devils: ye cannot be partakers of the Lord's table, and of the table of devils" (I Corinthians 10:14–20, emphasis added).

The physical cup represents a very real spiritual communion and participation with the Lord. Likewise, there are very real devils that are using rituals, idols, sacrifices, TVs, and drums to deceive men and lead them away from God and His holy nature. While it is true that meat, idols, TVs, and drums are amoral, it is also true that there can be a very real evil working through the messages communicated by rituals, idols, TVs, and drums.

Although meat is amoral, God knows how Satan can use meat. Therefore God's anger was kindled against Israel when they ate sacrifices to idols in participation of heathen rituals: "And Israel abode in Shittim, and the people began to commit whoredom with the daughters of Moab. And they called the people unto the sacrifices of their gods: and the people did eat, and bowed down to their gods. And Israel joined himself unto Baalpeor: and the anger of the LORD was kindled against Israel"

(Numbers 25:1–3). "They joined themselves also unto Baalpeor, and ate the sacrifices of the dead. Thus they provoked him to anger with their inventions: and the plague brake in upon them" (Psalm 106:28–29).

The heathen, whether conscious of it or not, worship Satan and his demons. Paul's great concern for believers is that they not unknowingly have fellowship with devils! This same concern is expressed in the Old Testament: "They sacrificed unto devils, not to God; to gods whom they knew not, to new gods that came newly up, whom your fathers feared not" (Deuteronomy 32:17, see also Leviticus 17:7, II Chronicles 11:14–15, Psalm 106:37, and Revelation 9:20).

It is so easy for Christian liberty to become an occasion to the flesh: "For, brethren, ye have been called unto liberty; only use not liberty for an occasion to the flesh, but by love serve one another" (Galatians 5:13). Paul explained that along

> While it is true that meat, idols, TVs, and drums are amoral, it is also true that there can be a very real evil working through the messages communicated by them.

with the joy of great spiritual privileges comes the responsibility of watchfulness and self-control. Because Israel used their liberty as an occasion to the flesh, God was not pleased with them and overthrew many of them in the wilderness. (See I Corinthians 10:1–5.) Then Paul warned that what happened to Israel can very well happen to believers. (See I Corinthians 10:6–11.) This brought Paul to his conclusion: "Wherefore let him that thinketh he standeth take heed lest he fall" (I Corinthians 10:12).

If such caution and watchfulness are needed with amoral things such as meat, how much more are such caution and watchfulness needed with moral things such as music. Meat is merely a combination of physical elements that will one day melt with fervent heat. However, music is a language. It is capable of expressing the very nature of God and will exist in its purest form in the heart of God through eternity. Meat is a component of the temporal body. Music is an expression of the eternal character.

Satan is a deceiver who would love to infiltrate a worship service with untested music and mix the pure Word of God with unclean musical messages. Remember the principles of clean and unclean discussed in Chapter 6. Purity is not so readily communicated as impurity. The paths to sin are manifold; the paths to holiness one. One drop of filth will defile a vase of water; many drops of water will not purify a vase of filth. One bad apple will spoil the barrel, so don't mix them. As Paul says, "Ye cannot drink the cup of the Lord, and the cup of devils: ye cannot be partakers of the Lord's table, and of the table of devils" (I Corinthians 10:21). Recall from Chapter 8 how contemporary, worldly music originated from music that facilitates the possession of the worshippers by devils. The same kind of worldly music in the church would lead the church into carnality, quench the Holy Spirit, and facilitate God's judgment rather than a revival.

> If such caution is needed with amoral things such as meat, how much more is caution needed with moral things such as music.

In summary, Paul introduced a new fact in I Corinthians Chapter 10 after addressing idol worship in I Corinthians Chapter 8. I Corinthians 8 refers to the gods "believed by the worshippers" to be represented by the idols, gods that Paul recognized as not having any real existence. Therefore Paul shows tolerance for the consciences of those who abstain from eating meat offered to these idols. However, I Corinthians 10 is a different story. It refers to communion with real devils lurking behind the scenes, devils that delude the worshippers into false worship. Therefore Paul shows intolerance for participation in activities associated with the worship of devils, whether knowingly or unknowingly.

5. DEFINE A FAMILY STANDARD OF EXCELLENCE

Defining a family standard of music is an excellent opportunity for a father to show responsibility for spiritual leadership in the home. The ideal time to do this is when the children are young. As children become older, it is important to explain the Biblical basis for family standards so that they understand the desire to know Christ, which differs from a desire to "just follow rules." If our standards are Biblical, then God will confirm them in the hearts of our children as well.

For his birthday one year, our son wanted to play miniature golf. The first place we visited refused our appeal to turn off their music. I had taken the day off from work in the middle of the week, and there were no other golfers at the miniature golf course that day, but even so, they refused to turn off the music.

We decided to drive to another location even though it was much farther away. I was quite surprised to receive the same response to our second appeal. It was discouraging, but this feeling was eclipsed by an inner joy knowing that my son had chosen to remain faithful to the standards God had given our family, whatever the cost.

On our way home we passed a state park and pulled in to see if they had a miniature golf course. To our delight, they did. As we walked up to the fence we noticed that it was locked; no one was in sight. As we turned to leave, a park ranger happened to drive by and informed us that the miniature golf course at the park did not open for another month, on Memorial Day. However, when he learned about our son's birthday, he opened the gate, handed us golf balls and golf clubs, and showed us where to put them when we left!

> Standards keep us from the places where God does not want us to go, so that He can direct us to the places where He does want us to go.

So there we were on this beautiful spring morning on a well-kept course all to ourselves, surrounded by the sound of songbirds instead of loud worldly music, and—without cost! God sure knows how to set up a birthday party. But the way He set it up and directed us was through our standards in music.

God had this kind ranger waiting to offer us a wonderful birthday gift. But to get us to this place, God had to stop us from going to other places, which He accomplished through faithfulness to our music standard. Standards keep us from the places where God does not want us to go, so that He can direct us to the places where He does want us to go.

6. ESTABLISH A DISCIPLESHIP CLASS

"My people are destroyed for lack of knowledge: because thou hast rejected knowledge, I will also reject thee, that thou shalt be no priest to me: seeing thou hast forgotten the law of thy God, I will also forget thy children" (Hosea 4:6). Because of the prevalence of worldly music, there is a corresponding need to learn how to test the spirit of musical sound. Much could be done to teach the history and morality of music, along with other discipleship topics.

"Oh that my people had hearkened unto me, and Israel had walked in my ways! I should soon have subdued their enemies, and turned my hand against their adversaries. The haters of the Lord should have submitted themselves unto him: but their time should have endured for ever" (Psalm 81:13–15). There are many enemies and adversaries who truly hate the Lord and His church. The key to their decision to submit themselves to the Lordship of Christ, according to this passage, is simply for God's people to hearken to the Lord themselves and to walk in His ways. Instead of pridefully assuming that everything we are doing is right, the Church needs to periodically set aside times in which it seriously evaluates whether we are truly walking in God's ways. (Consider I Corinthians 11:26–28 and II Chronicles 7:14.) If God's ordinary people were living extraordinary lives in Christ without the addiction of worldly stimulants,

> ... the Church needs to periodically set aside times in which it seriously evaluates whether we are truly walking in God's ways.

we would be pure light and savory salt capable of drawing and preserving the lost the way God intended.

7. PROVE AND TRAIN SONG LEADERS

Just as there is a process of proving and approving of speakers in the church before they are given authority to influence the congregation, so a similar process should be set up to prove those who lead music in church. (See I Chronicles 15:16.) The Bible sets forth qualifications for spiritual leaders, because they are responsible for feeding and protecting the flock.

> There are times when saying nothing about the attacker or Goliath or unclean music would be cowardly.

If an evil man is attacking a child, we would stop the man—not because we hate him but because we love the child. When Goliath attacked the armies of God, David stopped him. (See I Samuel 17.) It may not be easy, but we are called to fight the good fight of faith. (See I Timothy 6:12.) We cannot remain silent. There are times when saying nothing about the attacker or Goliath or unclean music would be cowardly.

8. DEFINE A CORPORATE STANDARD OF EXCELLENCE

This recommendation is to apply to denominational policy that which has been proven and tested at the local level. The messages in ungodly music are attacking the Word of God. Satan wants to take the Scriptures out of our heart and consume our time with false substitutes such as music, sports, hobbies, etc.

Without any standard in the church there will be an unspoken and an untested standard that will fail to shield God's people from the lie that music is amoral and that any type of music is acceptable. We must always be vigilant in "proving what is acceptable unto the Lord" (Ephesians 5:10).

9. APPEAL TO LOCAL MERCHANTS

The customer is always right, so speak out. If a business is playing melodious music, make it a point to compliment them about the pleasant atmosphere they provide. Then ask to speak to the manager in order to personally thank him or her; managers do not hear praise very often. It also may be possible to write a short note of thanks on a Comment Card.

If a business is playing worldly music, politely ask the person in authority to turn it off, or ask to speak to the person who has the authority to turn it off. If he refuses, ask him to at least change the station or to turn down the volume. If he still refuses, another option is to leave.

> The power to stand alone is the heritage of those who are convinced that God's ways work.

Our family has also requested permission to play our personal CDs at roller skating rinks and ice skating rinks. Dare to be a Daniel; dare to stand alone. The power to stand alone is the heritage of those who are convinced that God's ways work. The Author of life offers to all of us a better way of life: ". . . I am come that they might have life, and that they might have it more abundantly" (John 10:10).

10. UNDERSTAND THAT THERE IS A LEGAL BASIS FOR A REFORMATION

Authorities are ordained of God to punish those who do evil and to praise those who do good: "For rulers are not a terror to good works, but to the evil. Wilt thou then not be afraid of the power? do that which is good, and thou shalt have praise of the same" (Romans 13:3). There is a proper time and a proper way to work with authorities to establish reforms. Two specific reforms to consider in relation to worldly music are (1) laws related to contributing to the delinquency of minors and (2) laws related to product liability.

Contributing to the Delinquency of Minors

Genuine love gives a person what they need not just what they want. Those who love their neighbor as themselves must never support those things that contribute to the delinquency of minors:

> Every state in America has laws to protect minors from those that would encourage them in any way to be delinquent. For example, any person who knowingly or willfully causes, aids, or encourages any boy or girl to be a delinquent child or who knowingly or willfully does acts which directly tend to render any such child so delinquent is guilty of the Class A misdemeanor of contributing to the delinquency of children. 720 ICLS Illinois Compiled Statutes 130/2A "Contributing to the delinquency of children," 1993.

A study of rock music is not complete without the recognition of its clear relationship to rebellion, drugs, immorality, and the occult. The connection between these destructive behaviors begins with alienation from parents, then association with others who are alienated from their parents, and finally a participation in activities that are promoted by the message or lyrics of the music.

This relationship [between rock music and delinquent behavior] was also identified by a committee of the American Medical Association and reported in the *Journal of the American Medical Association.* [2]

The legal question to consider is whether rock performers are aware that their music has an addictive effect upon the listeners. They should stop to consider what causes thousands of listeners in their audiences to lose personal inhibitions and allow the music to control their actions with screaming, dancing, and a continuing, insatiable desire for the rock beat.

How to Conquer the Addiction of Rock Music continues: "These performers would be quick to claim that they do not cause the unlawful actions of young people. However, the law is concerned with a wider scope of responsibility. The question of the law is, 'Do these performers or promoters do anything to contribute to factors which encourage young people to become delinquent?'"

> The legal question to consider is whether rock performers are aware that their music has an addictive effect upon the listeners.

Product Liability

Those who love the Lord Jesus Christ and desire His will to be done on earth as it is in heaven must support product liability laws:

Because of the testimonies of users and the damages and injuries incurred by rock addiction, those who produce or sell rock or rap music should be aware of product-liability laws.

Product-liability laws protect consumers from harmful or defective products or products that do not sufficiently warn the user of unseen dangers. These laws also provide for compensation to those who have been harmed by such products.

If rock music is purchased by someone who is not aware that it has an addictive nature, and if that person becomes addicted to rock music by listening to it and damage occurs as a result of his addiction, those who produced or sold the music should be liable for the damage that occurred to the user.

There are three requirements for a plaintiff to establish liability on the producers or distributors of a product:

(1) There was action, whether intentional or negligent, taken by the producers or distributors of the product which made the product more dangerous than the consumer was aware.

(2) An injury occurred to a user of the product.

(3) There is a direct link between the injury incurred and the product itself (causation). [3]

The addictive rock beat that has been added to music has caused psychological and physical harm to many young people as a direct result of drugs, immorality, or alienation from parents. Producers or distributors of rock music should [be compelled by law to] place warning labels on their tapes and compact disks telling of the dangers of addiction by listening to their music. [4]

There came a time in dealing with unreasonable religious leaders when Paul had to appeal to civil leaders: "But when the Jews spake against it, I was constrained to appeal unto Caesar; not that I had ought to accuse my nation of" (Acts 28:19). If believers do not take a stand now, evil will prevail to the point that we will not be able to stand later. When Goliath arose and came toward David, David hasted and ran toward Goliath: "And it came to pass, when the Philistine arose, and came and drew nigh to meet David, that David hasted, and ran toward the army to meet the Philistine" (I Samuel 17:48).

Now is the time to stand! If necessary, now is the time to stand alone! ". . . Now is the day of salvation" (II Corinthians 6:2).

ENDNOTES: SECTION IV

Chapter 10

1 *How to Conquer the Addiction of Rock Music*, IBLP, 1993, pp. 81–85

2 www.cbsnews.com/2100-207_162-3230264.html

3 *How to Conquer the Addiction of Rock Music*, IBLP, 1993, p. 94

4 *How to Conquer the Addiction of Rock Music*, IBLP, 1993, pp. 13–14

5 Stephen Maphosah, Zimbabwe, Africa, printed in *What the Bible Has to Say About . . . Contemporary Christian Music*, p. 8

6 *Advanced Seminar Textbook*, IBLP, 1986, p. 138

7 *The Life and Times of Little Richard*, by Charles White, p. 197

Chapter 11

1 *How to Conquer the Addiction of Rock Music*, IBLP, 1993, pp. 15–17

2 *How to Conquer the Addiction of Rock Music*, IBLP, 1993, pp. 78–80

3 William P. Statsky, Torts: Personal Injury Litigation 494–503, 1982

4 *How to Conquer the Addiction of Rock Music*, IBLP, 1993, pp. 90–91